www.IAmCollegeMaterial.com

Josh-
Thanks for participating in this project. Your contribution is invaluable. Godspeed, Zach

I AM COLLEGE MATERIAL!

YOUR GUIDE TO UNLIMITED
COLLEGE, CAREER, AND LIFE SUCCESS

Zach Rinkins

Australia
PUBLISHING

I Am College Material! Your Guide to Unlimited College, Career, and Life Success

Copyright © 2017 by Zachary R. Rinkins

All rights reserved. No part of this book may be reproduced or transmitted in any form or by any means without written permission from the author.

ISBN-10:0-9994022-0-X
ISBN-13:978-0-9994022-0-7

Library of Congress Control Number: 2017914170

Printed in the USA by Australia Publishing

Formatted by A.Nicole by Design, LLC.

DEDICATION

"Education is as essential to biology as food."
— **W. Montague Cobb, M.D., Ph.D.,**
Anatomist, Historian, and Anthropologist

I dedicate this book to students and the army of people that support them. You will contribute to 100 percent of our future.

ACKNOWLEDGEMENTS

There are no self-made people. We are shaped by God's generous blessings and the love and contributions of others. I have certainly benefitted from an army of supporters.

First, I express profound gratitude to my wife Roshell Rosemond Rinkins, MBA, the woman who inspires, supports, and loves me unconditionally. Thank you for riding with me on our journey of life and romance.

To my mother Denise Rinkins, who gave me her absolute best, thank you for being the first person to believe in me and love me unconditionally.

To my late grandmother, Merletta Gordon Rinkins, my eternal example of love, dignity, determination, and endurance; to Michelangelo Whitehead, thank you for inserting yourself into my life and being a father to me; my uncles Michael and Australia Rinkins; my godparents Betty and Alvin Miller; my cousins Dorothy and Willie Sellers who took care of me while I attended college; Ivey L., the late Marie, Johana, Ivy-Victoria and Rose Williams, for adopting me into your family.

To all of the people and subject matter experts I have interviewed over the years for various media outlets and the people who generously shared their insights and wisdom, you breathe life into this book.

To my copy editors: Jo Ann Jones, J.D., Courtney Kambobee, M.Ed., Avarian McKendrick, J.D., and Yanela G. McLeod, Ph.D., you all helped me discover and refine my voice.

To my educators: Adeline Evans, Ph.D., the late James Hawkins, Ph.D., former dean of Florida A&M University School of Journalism & Graphic Communication, William Jiles, M.A., Kenneth Jones, MFA, Henry L. Lewis, III, Pharm.D., Keith Miles, Joseph Ritchie, M.A., Valerie White, Ph.D., and Gale Workman, Ph.D., thank you for challenging me and helping me to see my possibilities.

To my various mentors and supporters: Herbert Ammons, Jr., Dexter A. Bridgeman, MPA, Vincent T. Brown, J.D., Tina Dupree, Ph.D., Alfred Edmond, Jr., Trenae Floyd, W. Steven Green, Larry Hunt, M.Div., Robert Lemon, Rel.D., Bernard C. Poitier, Sr., Melvin F. Sabree, Sr., A.P., Jeffrey D. Swain, J.D., Ph.D., and Donald L. Thompson, Sr. – thank you.

To Saint Matthews Missionary Baptist Church in Miami, Florida; Redeemed Christian Church of God–International Chapel in Tallahassee, Florida; and the Baptist Collegiate Ministry at Florida A&M University, thank you for the continued love and spiritual support.

TABLE OF CONTENTS

LIST OF TABLES

1. Emerging Professional vs. College Student. 5
2. Seven Advantages of Group Studying 29
3. Top 10 Most Popular Majors, Top 10 Least Popular Majors 44
4. Top 10 Undergraduate Majors with Highest Median Earnings ... 46
5. Top 10 Undergraduate Majors with Lowest Median Earnings 47
6. Top 10 Majors with Highest Employment Rates 48
7. Top 10 Majors with Highest Unemployment Rates 49
8. IACM College Student Budget 62
9. Credit Score Ranges 68
10. Five Credit Score Categories 69
11. IACM College Student Money Challenges 70
12. IACM Mind, Body, and Soul Action Items 92
13. Boundaries for Safe and Healthy Relationships 97
14. Qualities of a Healthy Relationship 100
15. Domestic Abuse Warning Signs 110
16. IACM Safety Suggestions 113
17. Seven Must Have Skills to Get Hired 118
18. Scheffer and Rubenfeld's Seven Critical Thinking Skills 121
19. IACM Professional Values for Career Success 123
20. IACM Elements of Professional Work Execution 124
21. Lindsay Olson's 10 Top Communication Tips 131
22. Jeff Bernoff's 10 Top Writing Tips 134
23. IACM Internship Action Plan 149
24. Job Offer Rates and Starting Salaries by Internship and Co-Op Experience 151
25. Top Global Economies 157
26. Four Must Have Resources for Effective Networking 175

CHAPTER 1
INTRODUCTION: START STRONG

> 66 *"Education is the passport to the future, for tomorrow belongs to those who prepare for it today."*
>
> — **Malcolm X,** Human Rights Leader 99

What does it mean to be educated in the 21st century? During my time as a college administrator at a private university, a recurring experience served as the motivation for this book. It goes something like this:

Excited Young Person: Hey Mr. Rinkins, I am about to graduate. Thanks for all your help.

Me: I am thrilled for you. You overcame everything in your way and made it to this moment. Congratulations!

Excited Young Person: Yes, sir!

Me: What's next for you?

Excited Young Person: I am going to be a manager at a rental car location, mobile phone franchise, or work at a local community center.

Me: Great!

Excited Young Person: Thanks for all your help.

Wow! During various conversations with students over a few commencement periods, my heart would break. I would literally break down into tears. Why? Because I know the majority of these students spent approximately $77,240 — with interest in most cases — to pursue a job that might pay them $28,000 a year. I know their families did not send them to college to become one of the 22 million Americans whom *Wall Street Journal* reports are not paying or cannot repay their student loans.

Some economists say many of those former college students may never be able to payback student loans. These students deserve so much better than falling into an unfulfilling and low-paying career. Malcolm X might ask, "For what future did these young people prepare themselves?"

I Am College Material! is designed to help you succeed as you work to gain a useful understanding of the college experience to create the quality of life you deserve. This book is written as a manual to help students develop an action plan to get the most out of their college experience. Insights from more than 50 subject-matter experts will enable you to benefit from their wisdom instead of trying to figure it out on your own.

I Am College Material! is both a declaration and commitment to using the college experience to transform yourself into the person you desire to be. The sole purpose of the book is to give readers a competitive advantage in college, career, and life.

It is hard to work on a college campus and not become attached to students. You get the chance to see some students start as bright-eyed freshmen and transform into young adults ready to dominate the world before them. It is very fulfilling to experience and contribute to their evolution. The author has lived through virtually every aspect of the college experience. These experiences include living both on- and off campus; being on academic probation as well as the dean's list; being debilitatingly depressed during college; going from being a college student to enjoying employment as a college administrator, and everything in between. The data, resources, and interviews included in this writing are aimed to serve you.

Human rights leader Malcolm X said, "Education is the passport to the future, for tomorrow belongs to those who prepare for it today." If we take Minister Malcolm's logic, we can assert that those who do not educate themselves have a passport to nowhere. Tomorrow will never belong to them because they have not mastered today through steadfast preparation.

Merriam-Webster   Dictionary   New   Edition   (Merriam-Webster, Inc.) defines educate as "developing mentally, morally, or aesthetically, especially by instruction." That definition comes close to the essence of what it means to be educated.

If we were honest with ourselves, we would realize education is ambiguous. With each day and new experience, life gives us an opportunity to educate ourselves. It is truly what we make of it. We have to define education for ourselves. Our respective futures depend on it.

***

Wake UP! Emerging Professionals vs. College Students

❝ *"In essence, your goal is to acquire an education, not a diploma, because you are worth more than a piece of paper; an education, not a job, because you deserve better than that."*

— **Zach Rinkins**, Author, Journalist ❞

You may have heard the story of the fictional character Rip Van Winkle. Celebrated essayist Washington Irving introduced us to Rip in *The Sketch Book* (Dodd, Mead & Company). The story is set in the Catskill Mountains during the American Revolution. Rip Van Winkle is a man who procrastinates on his responsibilities and squanders his young adult life and strength on unproductive pursuits, drinking alcohol, and playing games.

Rip falls asleep one day and wakes up 20 years later. After he awakes, he realizes that so much around him has changed. The Americans won the Revolution, his nagging wife is dead, and only his daughter recognizes him and takes him in. He eventually resumes his past purposeless behavior as the world around him evolves and moves on. **DO NOT GRADUATE AS RIP VAN WINKLE!**

Wake up! You are not a college student! Erase that philosophy from your mind. College students believe that their education is someone else's job. That approach only produces regret, disappointment, and low self-esteem. You are an emerging professional. Emerging professionals take ownership of their education and take responsibility for everything concerning their future. They understand that taking responsibility does not mean that everything is their fault. It means they personally take action to respond to everything regarding their life and wellbeing. This approach produces results, fulfillment, and high self-esteem. The way you start your education has a long-term impact on your future.

You want to maximize your college experience to help create the life you deserve. There are very few times in life where you can solely concentrate on improving yourself, so don't waste this opportunity daydreaming about times when life was easier or hanging out with unproductive peers.

Are you an emerging professional? An emerging professional understands they do not know everything. They are, however, willing to do what it takes to find out how they can learn what they need to know. These individuals are always evolving and mastering the challenges set before them, they develop confidence and earn the respect of their peers. Or, are you a college student?

College students procrastinate and never overcome the lessons needed to move ahead in life. Their peers have little confidence in them and their abilities. And, they remain unsure themselves.

Rip Van Winkle was present, but he did not have a presence. Being present and having presence can be the difference between being ordinary and extraordinary. Be mindful that your start has a tremendous influence on how you finish. Gaining a real education is the ability to look at the world, see challenges and trends, and use information and resources to create solutions to those challenges. Doing so will advance your personal and community ambitions. The revolution will not be handed to you. It's time to wake up, show up, and take your rightful place in the world! **You are COLLEGE MATERIAL!**

EMERGING PROFESSIONAL VS. COLLEGE STUDENT

Emerging Professional Attitudes and Actions	College Student Attitudes and Actions
Acquires marketable skills.	Believes learning is the teacher's job.
Participates in class.	Goes to class.
Immediately starts building contacts.	Tries to make contacts during their senior year.
Gains experience through internships, professional organizations, and volunteer opportunities.	Takes the summer off or accepts unchallenging internships that do very little to advance their career.
Attracts opportunities for advancement.	Acquires unnecessary debt.
Travels internationally.	Wants to have unproductive fun.
Has many opportunities from which to choose.	Pursues or accepts unfruitful jobs with low-pay and low outlooks.
Builds self-confidence and earns peers' respect.	Unsure of themselves and has a "nobody ever helps me," mentality.
Creates the opportunity of a lifetime.	Hopes to get it together.

Table 1.

CHAPTER 2
THE DIARY OF AN EMERGING PROFESSIONAL

❝ *"It is not your environment; it is you — the quality of your mind, the integrity of your soul and the determination of your will — that will decide your future and shape your life."*
— **Benjamin E. Mays, Ph.D.**, Scholar, Education Leader ❞

***

Why are you here? Stay focused!

If you were a student at South Carolina State University (SCSU) and walked into the offices of Joseph Thomas, SCSU's career services director, he would immediately challenge you by asking:

- Why are you here?
- What is your purpose?
- Why are you advancing your education?

Thomas, who has been employed for nearly 30 years in student services, offers a wise observation:

"When you make the transition from high school to college, it is a culture shock. You think you are ready, but you begin to see students that are just as smart or smarter than you are. Then we put a whole lot of information before you. It can be information overload as you are adjusting to a new environment and gaining new friends."

The SCSU alumnus offers this guidance:

"Students must become aware of everything around them. They must keep their goals before them and avoid all distractions. There are so many distractions in college. These four years go by so quickly. Stay focused and accomplish your goals."

Emerging professionals stay focused, so they do not have to get focused.

***

Students of the Game: Learning the Rules of Engagement

> " *"The function of education is to teach one to think intensively and to think critically. Intelligence plus character – that is the goal of true education."*
>
> — **Martin Luther King, Jr., Ph.D.**, Theologian, Human Rights Activist "

Students who approach college as emerging professionals realize that to master any situation they must invest the necessary time to learn the rules and policies of their environments. They take time to discover helpful people around them and university resources like the Student Handbook and College Catalogue. These documents are useful tools for developing a plan to navigate their academic environment.

The student handbook is a resource that spells out the rules, rights, and punishments related to students. Sometimes called the school's "Rules, Policies, and Procedures" book, this resource explains the school's expectations of students, provides policies related to student rights, and outlines penalties for inappropriate behavior.

The College Catalogue is one of the most valuable resources on campus because it includes the credentials, abbreviated resumes, and professional accomplishments of faculty and staff. Students can also view the undergraduate and graduate alma maters, research publications, and in some cases previous jobs of faculty and staff as well. Having this information can help you learn the research and professional interests of your professors, advisers, and school department chairpersons. You also seek this information by searching LinkedIn profiles and scholar.google.com for faculty and staff members in your academic department.

An excellent navigation tool, you can use the catalog to find out which campus employees attended schools or worked at organizations that interest you. Developing fruitful relationships with staff that are alumni of institutions on your graduate and professional schools wish list could prove helpful during the admissions process. Do your research and schedule a courtesy appointment with the contact to plant seeds for fruitful relationships (See: Networking 101).

***

You Belong in College: Acquiring a Sense of Belonging

" *"I had to make my own living and my own opportunity, but I made it! Don't sit down and wait for the opportunities to come. Get up and make them."*
— **Madame C.J. Walker**, America's First "
Female Self-Made Millionaire

Never let anyone or anything make you feel as if you do not belong at your university. Thousands of people applied for admission into your school. Remember, you were chosen. Well-known educational diversity scholar Terrell Strayhorn, Ph.D., reveals that gaining a sense of belonging does not come automatically. You have to acquire it. The college professor says it takes hard work to create campus connections. He recommends students start the process by learning more about their schools and establishing campus relationships.

"True membership goes to those who understand the place to which they want to belong," offers Dr. Strayhorn, author of *College Students' Sense of Belonging: A Key to Educational*

Success for All Students (Routledge). "If you want to feel like you belong at a school, you must know something about it."

The Do Good Work, LLC, (www.DoGoodWorkLLC.org) founder likens it to the Greek fraternity and sorority pledging process. "I'm in a fraternity. I feel like a bonafide member. The reason I know that I am a member is because I know the organization's history, traditions, customs, and practices. I also have meaningful, deep relationships with some of its members," continues Strayhorn, who says the metaphor applies to college students. He notes:

> "You will never have a sense of connection or belonging if you don't know anything about your school's history. You don't have to know the entire history, but knowing something helps you decide your role in shaping your school's present and future."

Dr. Strayhorn encourages students to develop and maintain relationships with fellow students, faculty and staff members. He encourages students to be open to developing new relationships, trying new things, and attending university events. Dr. Strayhorn concedes that his relationship skills were lacking during his first year at the University of Virginia (UVA).

"When I came to UVA, the cultural center would pair students with a high-achieving student. I was paired with Carmen. I had no intention of meeting her, even if she had plans for meeting me," he recalls. "I thought I could just come to college and work hard; get good grades, and graduate, much like high school. I never thought about the importance of relationships."

Dr. Strayhorn admits he ignored Carmen's many invitations to university events. After several unanswered emails, he heard a knock on his door.

"Carmen comes to my residence hall and says, 'There is a cookout, and I invited you. So since you're here, you're coming,'" he remembers. "I said, 'no I'm not coming.' She literally took my hand and took me to the cookout, and I had a blast!"

He explained the friendly intervention improved his college experience. He shares, "I met other UVA students whom I would not have met otherwise. They were high achieving and academically focused like me. Before you know it, I was building the relationships that were responsible for me feeling a sense of belonging, but that took my peer mentor snatching me out of my dorm to go."

***

Personal Development: Building Self-Esteem

❝ *"The thing you fear most has no power. Your fear of it is what has the power. Facing the truth really will set you free."*

— **Oprah Winfrey**, Billionaire, Multimedia Mogul ❞

Self-esteem is not given to you at birth. It is something you build. It can come from only one place, your behavior. At age 18, Francine Ward, J.D. spiraled into a life of substance abuse, promiscuity, and low self-esteem. At age 26, she said goodbye to alcohol, drugs, and prostitution, and a decade later the high school dropout said hello to a juris doctorate from Georgetown University Law Center. She says building self-esteem helped her create a life beyond her wildest imaginations.

In her book, *Esteemable Acts: 10 Actions for Building Real Self-Esteem* (Crown), Ward writes: "Believe it or not, your behavior determines your feelings about you. Self-esteem is built on doing things that genuinely make you feel good about yourself, things that always give you an opportunity to walk through something you are afraid of. Stay focused on what you say is important to you."

The San Francisco-area attorney says you can build self-esteem by consistently fulfilling the promises you have made to yourself. When you enrolled in college, the world assumed that education was important to you. Make sure your habits, decisions, and how you spend your time reflect your priorities.

Use Ward's guidance to create small goals that will eventually have a significant impact on how you view yourself.

One college professor says doubting yourself will not help you accomplish anything. "Some students struggle with self-defeating attitudes," discloses Dr. Terrell Strayhorn. "I don't understand why so many college students assume that their peers are smarter than them. Focus on your strengths. Stop agonizing on your weaknesses. Success comes to those who maximize their strengths."

Price Cobbs, M.D., says, "If there is hopelessness inside, then you want to break the situation into small pieces." The Meharry Medical College-trained physician says this approach makes situations manageable and less intimidating.

"Ask yourself, what is my motivational message to myself? What can I say to myself to empower me to take the first step? After you take the first step, you can take the second step," implores Dr. Cobbs, a former assistant clinical professor of psychiatry at the University of California-San Francisco School of Medicine. "Unless you empower yourself to make the first step, your hopelessness will envelope you."

It takes hard work to build a positive inside voice that encourages and pushes you to do the things that are important to you. If you continue to hear a negative or discouraging voice, then make an appointment with a counselor to help you create a plan to cultivate a positive and encouraging voice (See: Mind, Body, and Soul).

***

Practice to Perfect: Cultivating a Professional Acumen

> " *"The difference between ordinary and extraordinary is practice."*
> — **Vladimir Horowitz**, Acclaimed Pianist, Composer "

High performing students know that one of the best ways to cultivate a professional acumen is to devote at least 3.5 hours

(30 minutes a day) each week to becoming well read about their intended industries. If you want to capture a key industry player's attention, you must have something interesting to say. The best way to create engaging conversations is to prepare for them by immersing yourself in current events, industry trends, and general news. Read, log-on or watch the following outlets:

- **NEWSWEEK OR TIME MAGAZINE:** These magazines provide a general analysis of newsworthy events each week. They post timely features at www.newsweek.com and www.time.com.

- **THE JOURNAL OF A DEFINITIVE ACADEMIC INSTITUTION:** In your major, these are published at various times depending on the institution, for example, *Journal of Applied Psychology* (American Psychological Association). The studies and articles published in journals eventually become cited sources in news reports and academic research. Even if you read only the abstracts, you will be more prepared than virtually all of your peers who never read or heard of these publications.

- **NEWS.GOOGLE.COM:** This platform separates timely information into top news, national news, business news, sports updates, technology trends, and local news.

- **60 MINUTES:** The most-watched newsmagazine in America. It features hard-hitting investigative reports, interviews, feature segments, and profiles of newsworthy people. Find out more information at www.cbsnews.com/60-minutes/.

- **USA TODAY:** The country's most popular daily newspaper featuring timely stories on current and national events and topics. You can access stories on its website at www.usatoday.com.

- **NATIONAL PUBLIC RADIO (NPR)**: The nation's only publicly supported radio network. Its programming tends to be less politically slanted or socially biased compared to commercial outlets. NPR has a program stream and archives its broadcasts at www.npr.org.

- **PUBLIC BROADCASTING SYSTEM (PBS)**: The nation's only publicly supported television network. "Talk of the Nation" and "Morning Edition" are among its most popular programs. Like NPR, this outlet also strives to present news from a politically neutral perspective.

- **INDUSTRY TRADE PUBLICATIONS AND ONLINE RESOURCES**: Consume insightful information from the blogs, websites, podcasts, and experts that cater to your academic major or desired industry. This information helps you stay up-to-date on issues and trends affecting your industry. Also, peruse the monthly periodicals of your professional organizations, newsletters, e-zines, and annual reports of organizations where you may want to work.

Being able to converse with confidence about general news and events in your industry will show that you are serious, knowledgeable, and employable.

***

Should I Live On-Campus?

Emerging professionals are more likely to live on-campus so they can enjoy greater overall satisfaction with their college experience and greater academic success than students who live off-campus.

"I wish I had stayed on campus," says Kelly Hunter, when asked about his college experience. "Because all of the resources are close to you or within walking distance. It puts you in a scholastic mindset."

According to the Association of College and University Housing Officers-International (ACUHO-I), students who live on campus enjoy higher academic performance, are more likely to graduate on time, are more apt to be exposed to people of other cultures, and have a greater self-esteem. M. Keener Scott, Ed.D., associate director for Staff Development and Student Conduct for the multiple award-winning Department of Housing at the University of Georgia (UGA), concurs.

"Students who live on campus have better grades and have a better transition from their parents' home to being on their own," says Dr. Scott, who is also the Inclusion and Equity Director of ACUHO-I. "They also develop a greater sense of community, which is invaluable while they are in college. Student housing promotes comfort and healthy relationships."

Dr. Scott, a 30-year student housing veteran, says living on campus can help students create a more successful college experience.

"Students need more support than they may realize," she continues. "We do that by supporting all the needs of students, not just beds and showers, but academically, socially, and even employment sometimes. Ultimately, having that experience makes you a better citizen."

Many colleges offer a variety of housing options for various types of students including: first-time college students, upperclassmen, graduate students, family housing, honors housing, and even major-based housing.

Dr. Scott tells students seeking to live in premium student housing to apply as early as possible. "The newer housing with modern amenities sometimes has a higher cost," she explains. "Some housing is based on academic major and academic performance. The students who get into the most desirable housing situations often apply early."

***

Off-Campus Living Considerations

When making the decision to live off-campus, consider some potential pitfalls to avoid when residing beyond campus perimeters. Hunter is an example of a student who, more than a decade after graduating, still regrets moving off-campus. Hunter, who earned a bachelor's degree in Hospitality Management from Bethune-Cookman University (BCU), says the choice brought on many unforeseen consequences.

"Moving off-campus was the single worst decision I made in my college career because I created an unnecessary burden that I was not ready for," Hunter laments. "I should have put myself in an environment that was entirely academic. Instead, I was trying to be independent."

Although the goal, independence has its price if crucial considerations are not carefully measured. Excessive obligations can include juggling unreliable transportation, roommate personalities and their vices, and other fluctuations of life off-campus.

"Sometimes you have to deal with being hungry, managing bills, roommates and their trash. Then, you're trying to catch the bus or find rides to work and school when your car is not working," he adds. "At least on campus, you have a meal plan and can just walk to class or the library."

Managing those additional obligations also meant Hunter would have to finance them with a job and more student loans. "I ended up having to maintain a full-time job and a full-time course load," concludes Hunter, who is a Charlotte-based educator and owner of www.KingofFoods.com. "It was difficult to just focus on school, which was why I came to college."

Hunter says moving off-campus increased his student loans by more than five figures and extended his time in college by two additional years. Plus, he had to take two separate semesters off.

***

Strategies for Off-Campus Living

If you still choose to move entirely off-campus with roommates, please consider these seven tips before signing the lease:

- **BE SAFE AND ECONOMICAL:** Move to a safe and economically realistic apartment or residence that is close to campus. Many college towns have affordable student-oriented apartments. Some offer roommate settings that are similar to dorms. These situations are ideal because many feature all-inclusive rent that includes all or most utilities (power, water, Wi-Fi, etc.). These types of rental agreements can be great because they often limit credit and bill exposure, meaning if one roommate does not pay their rent, the other roommates may not suffer power outages or adverse credit consequences.

- **INVESTIGATE POTENTIAL ROOMMATES:** Make sure your roomy is not a criminal. Perform a Google search of your prospective roommate. Then, check your local courthouse records (campus location) and your potential roommate's hometown courthouse records for criminal activity. Taking this step can prevent you from being housed with a reported sex offender or dangerous criminal.

- **GET SEPARATE MAILBOXES:** Have your mail sent to a trusted family member's home (if possible) or register for a post office box. Your mail can include bills and other correspondence that contain your social security number and other sensitive information, having a separate mailbox can help you avoid identity theft.

- **PROTECT YOUR CREDIT:** Each roommate should have the same credit exposure. Do not use your name or expose your credit to all of the bills. Make sure everyone's name is on the lease. Share the exposure. Credit issues can affect future employment opportunities and make your life more expensive (See: Dollars and Cents: Financial Literacy).

- **BUY A LOCK FOR YOUR ROOM DOOR**: Having a separate lock for the door to your room maintains your privacy, safety, and prevents identity theft.

- **R-E-S-P-E-C-T**: Respect your roommates' space and property. If you have any issues, talk it out like respectful adults. Do not scream and loudly criticize roommates over the phone to other people.

- **LIMIT HOUSEGUESTS**: It is not necessary to host all of your friends at your home, or have people know where you live for that matter. Limiting guests prevents precarious situations, identity, property theft, and maintains privacy.

***

Speaking the Language of Success

> *"Bilingual is someone who speaks two languages. Trilingual is someone who speaks three languages. What do you call someone who can only speak one language? An American."*
> — **Popular Joke** (Unknown)

"Many of our young people are city and neighborhood focused. It's not good enough to be the best student on their campus or even the best student in the country," proclaims Makola M. Abdullah, Ph.D., president of Virginia State University (VSU).

The leaders of tomorrow are not satisfied with being the best students in their major or on their campus. They know America has only 5 percent of the world's 7.4 billion population, according to the Population Reference Bureau's "2016 World Population Data Sheet." They understand they are only one person in a global pool filled with billions of willing and capable candidates.

Many international candidates have similar life experiences and educational accomplishments as their American counterparts. Unlike their American counterparts, many of our international brothers and sisters are often multilingual and speak languages of the emerging countries where many companies are trying to start or expand operations. This creates a significant competitive advantage for them (See: International Assignments).

A recent U.S. Labor Bureau Statistics report reveals foreign-born residents occupy nearly 15 percent of the American workplace. This reality, combined with the recent educational, economic, and technological advances around the world has given more people access to American colleges, jobs, and entrepreneurial opportunities. Emerging professionals learn other languages to level the corporate playing field.

"We cannot view ourselves as only American citizens," continues Patrick Anthony Williams, Ph.D., a foreign language instructor and polyglot. "We are citizens of the world. We (Americans) don't view other languages as a means of survival. We see them as a requirement to graduate from school. That type of thinking makes it hard for students to learn the language thoroughly."

Omar Goff, MBA, satisfied his curiosity for foreign languages and cultures during a 10-month internship in Brazil (See: International Assignments: Your Passport to Success). Goff maximized the opportunity by using the country's language and totally immersing himself in the local culture. "In Brazil, English was a luxury, so I had to learn Portuguese to do my work," he recalls. "I forced myself to learn the language. I requested that my co-workers only speak to me in Portuguese. I also listened to Portuguese music and watched Portuguese movies and television shows."

Goff says communicating in the country's language enhanced his immersion experience:

> "Speaking a person's native language allows you to be invited into their world. It also shows a level of business sophistication and savvy. It certainly helps secure that

initial connection. Speaking another language also benefitted me personally. People invited me into their homes and became my family. My ability to communicate with others enhanced my social life because I was able to talk to people. I built lifelong relationships while I was in Brazil."

The trilingual Goff encourages students to have an open mind about the world, culture, and languages.

Dr. Williams, a Fulbright Memorial Fund Scholar to Japan, says cultural immersion can help you accomplish that goal. He adds, "In America, any language other than English is seen as a foreign language as opposed to a second language. We have to see it as a means of survival. The best way to learn a language is to live it."

He says having a mentality that views English as the only necessary language, produces a superiority complex that can create difficulties for students seeking to learn others languages and the instructors charged with teaching them. Dr. Williams uses a more hands-on, experiential approach to teaching languages. "I make my classes conversational as opposed to writing and conjugating verbs," he asserts. "Just think about it! When you were a child your parents did not teach you English by telling you 'let's conjugate verbs.' Your brain picked it up from listening to other people! I tell students to put themselves in environments where the desired language is spoken. You will not get confused. Your brain will pick it up and start acquiring the language."

***

Approaches to Acquiring Other Languages

- STUDY A LANGUAGE IN COLLEGE: Dr. Williams speaks seven languages and earned his undergraduate degree in Spanish. Goff says he took Spanish classes from sixth grade through college. Dr. Williams and Goff agree that a formal language curriculum is best supported with extensive language usage and cultural immersion.

- **EXPOSE YOURSELF TO OTHER LANGUAGES**: Goff remembers falling in love with other languages when he was exposed to French in the first grade. Dr. Williams first started experimenting with languages by greeting people in their native tongue. Seeing their positive reactions encouraged him to expand his foreign vocabulary.

- **CONSIDER THE BENEFITS**: Dr. Williams is a career educator, entrepreneur, and even earned money as a federal court translator. He attributes his many streams of income to mastering multiple languages. He says using other languages helps you serve more people, experience different cultures in a meaningful way, and enjoy more employment and entrepreneurial opportunities.

- **UTILIZE TECHNOLOGY**: There are many software and mobile applications that can help facilitate your journey to another language, including, among others: Rosetta Stone, Duolingo, and www.FluentIn3Months.com.

***

Benefits of Student Clubs and Organizations

College is your launching pad to your next opportunity. There are numerous on-campus and collegiate organizations that can help you expand your network. Professional and interest groups provide many advantages including professional development, networking, and helping you get in the loop of your desired industry. College administrator Barbara Inman, Ed.D., promises that if you organize your time properly, you will have more than enough time for social activities and campus organizations (See: Networking 101).

"We think it's important for students to have a life outside of their academic experiences," notes Dr. Inman, vice president for

Administrative Services and Student Affairs at Hampton University.

> "Doing so includes joining student organizations, which helps students develop leadership skills. We encourage students to get involved in department-oriented student clubs and organizations. For example, if their desired career is in psychology, joining the Psychology Club may be helpful. A department faculty member advises the organization and it helps students get to know their future peers. Students can also gain exposure to people practicing in their field of study, and it helps them develop relationships and job-related experiences."

Delatorro L. McNeal, II, M.S. points out that joining student clubs and organizations helped him strive to be his best. "Joining student groups allowed me to network and connect with so many different people on so many different levels," McNeal remembers. "Being a student leader pushed me and taught me leadership, servanthood, and humility. It also got me into so many doors, conferences, and events and connected me with many incredible organizations. Student leadership helps put you in environments where you can win."

***

Professional Clubs and Organizations

Professional clubs and organizations provide professional development opportunities through forums, workshops, and conventions. You can gain access to industry experts and other students affiliated with your vocation. They keep you aware of upcoming industry trends and professional opportunities including jobs, internships, scholarships, and fellowships. Membership also provides access to exclusive email listservs, association publications, and annual conventions. These valuable resources give you a competitive advantage over your peers who lack them.

You can leverage these resources to capitalize on opportunities. Join the local and national chapters of the professional affiliate associations for your intended industry. There are even versions of these groups that cater to ethnic, gender, sexual orientation, and other identities. *Encyclopedia of Associations: National Organizations of the U.S.* (Gale, Cengage Learning) is a listing that features the nation's professional and industry organizations. Gale directories can be found in print or online at your college or local library (See: Appendix A).

If your campus does not have a chapter of these organizations, you may consider the following options:

- COLLABORATE WITH OTHER CAMPUSES: Reach out and fellowship with a student chapter at another local or regional college.
- NETWORK WITH PROFESSIONALS: Find out if the organization has a local professional chapter and reach out to key players.
- BECOME AN ORGANIZATION FOUNDER: Contact the organization's national office and learn how to start a student chapter on your campus.

***

Maximize Your Membership

It is not sufficient to just become a member of these organizations. You have to brand yourself as a young, emerging professional. You can do this by developing an active presence within your local and national chapters.

On a local level, seek leadership positions through chapter task forces and initiatives. Use these opportunities as a chance to demonstrate your mastery of particular skills. Also, reach out to local experts in your industry and invite them to your student chapter meetings. These experts become resources and can offer your group insight on current events and trends within the industry.

Make sure you give these experts a care package that includes a thank you card, a school mug or t-shirt, and a certificate of appreciation. Then, you individually thank them for the insight and time with a personal thank you card. Include a small gift certificate for coffee or iTunes. You must keep in touch with these contacts.

You can also make an impact in your organization by doing something different. Raise money, start an annual contest, or create a small scholarship. Doing so will help you establish a legacy. All it takes is a $1,400 endowment to fund an annual $100 grand prize photojournalism contest or book scholarship. You can use crowd funding or bake sales to support it.

On a national level, develop a presence as an active member of your group's digital and social networking platforms. Twice a month submit helpful and relevant articles to the group's listserv, Facebook page, Twitter profile, and other social media sites. Try to get published on the group's website and periodical. Run for a national student leadership position. Doing this gives you credibility within your industry, makes you attractive to influential individuals, and starts establishing you as an industry player.

Social and political interest groups offer another networking opportunity. These clubs and organizations cater to issues that matter to you. The groups also provide opportunities for personal development.

***

Time Management

❝ *"Don't manage time. Manage priorities."*
— **Anonymous** ❞

Premier pupils know time is not money. Through trial and error, they have come to realize that time is more valuable than money. They understand you can recoup lost funds, but you cannot recover lost time. These pupils have also learned that everyone gets 10,080 minutes in a seven-day week. They are committed to maximizing every second.

"There is no such thing as time management. It is about self-management. To succeed at the level we want to succeed, you have to value your time," says Delatorro McNeal, II, a peak performance expert. "The more you value your time, the less likely you are to waste it. When you truly believe in yourself and value your time, you won't waste your time with anything or anyone."

VSU President Makola M. Abdullah says avoiding distractions is key to successful time management in college and life.

"Most people waste their time by not prioritizing and forgetting why they pursued an endeavor," says Dr. Abdullah, who earned a Ph.D. in engineering from the Northwestern University at age 24. "If one has gone to school to get an education, then everything one does should reflect that."

The Petersburg, Virginia-based educational executive recommends students use a time blocking approach for academics. "I tell students to go about their studies like a job. Consider putting in eight or nine hours per day, and don't go to your dorm room in-between classes. If you do that, you can have all the fun you want and not have to stay up late into the night studying."

McNeal, who earned all A's in undergraduate and graduate school, says it is important to structure your course load in a way that gives you time to process your priorities and complete assignments.

"You don't have to schedule your classes for every day of the week. I would schedule my classes for only Mondays, Wednesdays, and Fridays, or Tuesdays and Thursdays," McNeal offers. "I never scheduled my classes for every day of the week. On my off days, I would do my work. I found great balance by not going to class every day."

The Dallas, Texas-based entrepreneur says planning your time and organizing your workspace is both helpful and efficient.

"I encourage students to use a planner because it's hard to manage anything that you can't see," McNeal admits. "Often you can't see it, so you can't manage it. By seeing where I put my time, I was able to take it to the next level."

He adds, "Also, make sure you are organized. Clear off those spaces where you're working. You can get more things done and think clearer in less cluttered areas."

Mastering all of these qualities will put you in fighting shape to overcome the trials and triumphs of life, liberty, and the pursuit of your education.

CHAPTER 3
LIFE, LIBERTY, AND THE PURSUIT
OF AN EDUCATION

> 66 *"Success is no accident. It is hard work,*
> *perseverance, learning, studying, sacrifice, and most*
> *of all, love of what you are doing or learning to do."*
> — **Pelé**, Global Athletic Icon 99

Delatorro L. McNeal, II, arrived on the campus of Florida State University (FSU) committed to crushing his college experience. "When I went to college, I went there to hustle. My mom was a single mother. I went there with a mindset that I didn't want to make my collegiate experience difficult on my mom or be a burden to her," says McNeal, a renowned speaker and author of *The Rules of the Game in Action*. "I knew college was expensive, so I came to get in, rock out, and leave without much debt."

Within five years, the proud FSU Seminole accomplished his goal. He graduated summa cum laude with two degrees, a bachelor's degree in Interpersonal and Speech Communication, and a master's degree in Instructional Systems Design and Human Performance Enhancement, and he did it without accumulating student debt. He attributes a part of his academic success to clarity, commitment, and a desire to serve others.

"Peak performance comes down really to having very clear goals for yourself and pushing diligently towards those goals on a consistent basis," explains McNeal, the creator of the CrushUniversity.com platform. "It is also being intentional about helping other people. The more we help others, the more we grow and succeed."

***

Systems to Success

President Abdullah of Virginia State University says a student's number one job is to, "plot a course to perform well." This means there are no secrets to success, but there are systems that help you create success. Those systems are comprised of commitments, techniques, resources, and habits that can help you produce great results. All you have to do is discover the best system for you.

Self-evaluation testing is one way to find out which methods can work for you. Cherae Farmer-Dixon, DDS, dean of the School of Dentistry at Meharry Medical College, finds assessment examinations very helpful for her students.

"We require our students to perform a series of tests: a personality test, reading comprehension test, and an analytical reading evaluation, so we can identify strengths and weaknesses. Each student has one-on-one counseling with our educational support staff," Dr. Farmer-Dixon explains.

Your school may have a testing center or an educational development center that offers these helpful tests including the Myers-Briggs Type Indicator (MBTI) and a host of aptitude, personality, and skills assessment tests. You can use the results to create a system that will help you plot your course for success.

"Students may think that they have done well at other schools, but some students come with shortcomings," Dr. Farmer-Dixon continues. "This helps them to identify their strengths and weaknesses before classes even start. It is really designed to identify challenges and help us monitor those areas and connect the students to workshops to help them succeed."

"Some students are resistant, but after that first exam they come in and ask for help. If students are struggling and they don't come in voluntarily, we will require them to come in and get the help."

United Negro College Fund (UNCF) CEO Michael Lomax, Ph.D., agrees students must be intentional and aggressive about creating a solid academic foundation. Dr. Lomax advises:

"The first semester of college, the period between freshman week and midterms, is probably the single most important period to define the health and success of the student. Get it right at the beginning and you will have a successful experience. If you have failures or difficulties in that first six-week period, you rarely overcome those challenges. It is important to establish the right study habits, make the appropriate transition, find the resources on campus, and begin to stick to the environment. Mistakes and omissions in the first six weeks make it very difficult to recover later on."

***

Group Studying: Creating Your "A" Team

Jawanzaa Kunjufu, Ph.D., says more students could experience academic success if they approached their college education as a collaborative experience. "Too many of us think we have to study and do things by ourselves," laments Dr. Kunjufu, author of *Closing the Racial Academic Achievement Gap.* "Too many of us fail in college because we are afraid to find a study partner. Conversely, our friends at Harvard and Stanford are getting A's because they have a study partner and a tutor. Get help if you need it."

In "The Impact of Study Groups and Roommates on Academic Performance," a March 2015 article published in the *Review of Economics and Statistics* (MIT Press), authors Tarun Jain, Ph.D. and Mudit Kapoor, Ph.D., both of the Indian School of Business, reveal that informal social interaction and group study could improve academic performance. Other academic research notes that study groups are less useful if they do not have focus and purpose.

Louisiana State University's (LSU) Center for Academic Success identifies seven advantages of group studying (See: Table 2) LSU offers a free Study Group Starter Kit to help create a study group (See: Appendix B).

Martez Prince, Pharm.D., R.Ph., found the group study approach helpful while completing a rigorous six-year professional pharmacy doctorate program at the Florida A&M University (FAMU) College of Pharmacy and Pharmaceutical Sciences (COPPS).

SEVEN ADVANTAGES OF GROUP STUDYING
Helps Reduce Procrastination
Improves Understanding and Absorption of Information
Provides Learning From Different Perspectives
Improves and Develops New Study Skills
Provides Good Company
Minimizes Test Anxiety
Enhances Personal and Professional Skills
Table 2. SOURCE: LSU Center for Academic Success

"During my sophomore year, I was taking three science and two math courses at the same time," Dr. Prince reveals. "We created a reliable group of friends that were fun to hang out with that would keep us accountable. We made it a habit of studying every day for at least two-and-a-half hours."

The Fort Pierce, Florida native says creating syllabus-based study plans and mock tests helped group members successfully pass their classes.

"We put together a course outline and created a study plan for every test," he shares. "Some days we would study by ourselves in the same room. Other times we would study together. We quizzed each other and would ask each other sample questions for the test. We also talked about our grades on the test and would come up with a group average. We all wanted an A. If someone got a lower grade we would teach the concepts they didn't fully understand."

But, what happens if you study and still do not understand the concept? McNeal challenges you to put a personal spin on the information. "Make the information personal. Always ask yourself, 'how does this apply to me?' Try to figure out how you can create examples that you can relate to."

He also recommends strategically asking instructors for help. "I sat in the front row of all my classes," he explained. "After my classes were over, I stayed behind at least twice a week to talk to my instructor. I let them know what I thought of their presentations and gave them a compliment about how they delivered it."

He says this is a perfect time to admit your challenges and ask for guidance. "I would ask questions on things I was not clear about," he recalls. "For example, I would say these are the notes I took on the subject, but I am not clear on this concept. I'd ask if there was another metaphor or approach that might help me understand the concept a little better. I'd also use office hours."

***

Identifying Peer Mentors

Dr. Kunjufu recommends, "Every college student should have a peer mentor and be matched with an upperclassman," noting that doing so can help pupils gain insight on professors that can help you earn good grades. McNeal used this strategy to earn a perfect 4.0 Grade Point Average in undergraduate and graduate school.

"I'd ask upperclassmen, 'What's the key to Dr. Smith? Or, what's the secret to Dr. Johnson,'" McNeal discloses. "They would share things like, 'make sure you do the extra credit for Dr. Smith. Make sure you volunteer and speak up in Dr. Johnson's class. Or, make sure you never second-guess Dr. Reed in front of other students. If you do that you will be in trouble.' These upperclassmen gave me the keys to the kingdom to these professors."

***

Understanding Academic Performance

Dr. Farmer-Dixon, says excellent academic performance opens the doors to more educational and professional opportunities.

"We constantly tell our children to go to college," Dr. Farmer-Dixon observes. "Too many of them thought all they had to do was show up. They didn't get the whole message. Not only do you have to show up, but you also have to show out and perform. Part of that is doing your due diligence to find out the possibilities for yourself."

Dr. Abdullah adds, "You have to commit yourself to your goal. You have to be willing to invest the time necessary to learn something. When I was in college, my study partner and I would be willing to study for however long it took to get it."

Dr. Abdullah also explained building effective – not necessarily friendly – relationships with professors is an essential trait for success in school and life.

"Some students think they have to like a professor to learn from them," Dr. Abdullah declares. "Other students may think they have to like a major to perform well. Liking things is overrated! If one wants the job that comes with the major, then one has to pass the major. Your job is to plot a course to perform well."

You also have to be willing to do what it takes (both morally and ethically) to learn the information, even if that means asking for help or committing yourself to repeatedly practicing academic exercises over and over again.

Dr. Farmer-Dixon offers, "Excelling academically is not about being the best and the brightest. It's about being willing and determined to do whatever it takes to succeed. It's what I call stick-to-it-tiveness. I will take a hard worker anytime over a so-called smart person any day."

***

Study Strategies

In general, many educators would recommend studying for at least three hours for every hour you are in class. Others might suggest you read the required material three times to better retain the knowledge. Those methods may or may not work for you. Your job is to find the most efficient way that helps you perform well. McNeal points out that understanding your learning style and knowing the things that help you perform at your highest level can help you accomplish your goals. He also says there are no shortcuts.

"It sounds simple, but I read what my instructors told me to read," McNeal admits. "Some people buy books and hate to read them. So, I read. I was never a crammer. I only went to the library about ten times in five years. I just did my work and used office hours."

He also encourages students to make time to review prior information. "Right before class, I would take the time to review notes from the previous class so that I could refresh my brain and get ready for new content."

***

Taking on Tutoring

If students still find their course load challenging, Dr. Kunjufu suggests using resources within the Academic Affairs or Student Affairs offices to help gain a better understanding.

"Every student should have a tutor," Dr. Kunjufu points out. "Many students are guilty of not seeking one. Sometimes their ego won't allow them to admit that they need a tutor."

Virtually all schools offer free tutoring services and labs in a variety of subjects ranging from mathematics, sciences, and writing.

Your transcript will follow you throughout your educational life. This reality intensifies the importance of securing tutors and study groups if you need them.

In summary, you can enhance your academic performance by doing the following things.

- Sitting in the front row of your class
- Developing productive relationships with upperclassmen and professors
- Seeking an on-campus tutor
- Attending professor office hours
- Using effective learning and studying styles
- Reviewing course information on a regular basis

***

Preparing for Graduate or Professional School

Meharry's Dr. Framer-Dixon encourages students seeking to attend graduate and professional school to have a long-term study plan to successfully pass the standardized tests required for admission (See: Appendix B). "Getting into professional school is a highly competitive process," she admits. "Each year, we accept only 60 students out of 2,000 applicants."

Dr. Farmer-Dixon recommends students prepare for graduate school requirements as soon as they start taking classes.

"Whatever year you start taking your science courses, get a DAT (Dental Admission Test) review book or go online and download some DAT practice questions," she offers. "That way as you are going through your coursework, you can study the same topic in the DAT material."

"If you are studying biology and going over mitosis, meiosis, and chromosomes, set aside a couple of hours a week to look through practice exams and see how those same concepts are being approached on the exam. It could be two or three hours on a Saturday."

The dental school dean says the long-term study will give students a competitive advantage. "Over the course of three or four years of taking courses and prerequisite classes, you are reviewing for your tests and that gives you a better sense of what to expect on the exam." She continues, "So, the months before the exam you are reviewing instead of studying. That gives you a better chance for optimum performance."

Although this example is specific to prospective dental school candidates, you can use the same approach with relevant courses and test material related to your major, such as the Law School Admission Test (LSAT) for prospective law school students. (See: Appendix B)

IACM TEST PREPARATION OPTIONS/RESOURCES:
- KAPLAN: www.KapTest.com
- THE PRINCETON REVIEW: www.PrincetonReview.com
- BEAT THE GMAT: www.BeatTheGMAT
- UMBC TESTING CENTER: www.UMBCTraining.com
- GRE: gre.Magoosh.com

Ruby L. Perry, DVM, dean of the Tuskegee University College of Veterinary Medicine (TUCVM), suggests students join preparatory organizations as undergraduates.

"We've developed a pre-veterinary scholars program because we want to get undergraduate students ready to succeed in highly rigorous programs," Dr. Perry says. "Sometimes a student can have a 3.8 GPA, but if they didn't have a rigorous background, they might struggle in a professional program."

Tuskegee's veterinary school was founded in 1945 when there were only 10 in America. Today, it serves nearly 300 students and remains one of only 30 programs accredited by the Association of American Veterinary Medical Colleges in the country. Each year the veterinary school receives more than 200 applications and only accepts approximately 70 students.

It could also prove helpful to apply to summer pre-professional programs at the graduate schools on your wish list. Doing so will give you the opportunity to gain exposure to the program, build relationships with program influencers, and evaluate whether the institution is a good fit for you.

***

Poor Performance: Burning Academic Bridges

Life, education, technology and the economy are rapidly changing. Many economists project the average American will change careers several times in their lifetime. A recent Gallup poll says more than 60 percent of Millennials are open to a career change. Sometimes it is necessary to gain additional education credentials to compete for those opportunities. Performing at a high academic level and earning good grades helps students who decide to pursue graduate and professional degree opportunities in the future.

"If students have been out of school for a long time, they have to satisfy all prerequisite courses for admission to professional school," says Dr. Farmer-Dixon. "Or, they may consider pursuing an additional degree to prove they can compete in a rigorous academic environment and leverage that performance to apply for professional programs."

Dr. Perry of Tuskegee's veterinary medicine program says low academic performance makes that journey more challenging. "There are no alternative students," Dr. Perry reasons. "We have standards. If students don't meet those standards, we can't admit them. I would hate to admit an unprepared student because they won't likely pass our curriculum. Our tuition is too expensive."

Poor academic performance also makes education more expensive as institutions are less likely to extend scholarships, grants, and fellowships to students who are less liable to pass.

Dr. Perry adds, "We care about our students. We care about their success. We set the bar high. They have to meet to the bar. We don't want them to be in so much debt that they can't get a job because they can't pass the licensing exam."

When students cannot gain admission into traditional programs, sometimes they consider applying to non-traditional, for-profit, foreign and/or non-accredited schools (See: Appendix B). However, in nearly all cases, these institutions are more expensive — sometimes twice as much — than their accredited counterparts. Many of these schools lack industry credibility and many of their graduates earn less than graduates of traditional colleges. This decreases earning potential while increasing education costs.

Lastly, billionaire entrepreneur Mark Cuban said a balanced liberal arts education would be the most valuable commodity in the marketplace. With so much emphasis on science, technology, engineering, and mathematics, it may be helpful to take prerequisite classes for professional programs while you pursue your bachelor's degree. This way you have a more balanced education and expose yourself to courses that can prepare you for future educational and professional opportunities.

***

Overcoming Poor Academic Performance

Tim Talley, MBA graduated from one of Buffalo, New York's premier technical high schools. Tally, who passed an admissions test to enter the school, remembers feeling as if the computer electronics classes came naturally to him.

Talley recalls, "I did very well in high school. It came naturally to me. It wasn't necessary to bring books home. I did whatever work I had in school."

After his first semester as an electrical engineering student at the University of Rochester, Talley soon found out that college was not the 13th grade.

"I was at a disadvantage because I didn't know how to study," he remembers. "I never really had to study before. You may be able to get along like that for a while, but eventually, the complexity of the work goes up exponentially. If you have no clue how to study and what studying is all about, you are at a disadvantage."

President Abdullah has seen this scenario many times throughout his career. "College is hard, but not absurdly harder than high school. It is not that it's harder. It's faster. So, what happens is if you fall behind, you can't catch up." The VSU president offers:

> "I tell students to study as if their lives depended on it until their first test. Then you will have a better idea whether you are studying too much or just right. If you are studying too much, you can always back up. Students do the opposite. They study too little and then they have to catch up. At that point, it is too late. They are already in a hole."

Talley eventually found himself in that figurative hole; which caught the attention of his department chair. "I was struggling to the point that it wasn't long before I would have gotten thrown out of school," says Talley, who was a member of the school's track team. "The first thing was the department chairman telling me to drop out because I would never make it."

Tally says the chair told him to save his parents' money, drop out of school, and become an electrician.

> "Eventually I had to grow up. I didn't ask my parents what I should do. That summer after my freshman year, I had to come home and decide what I was going to do. I had to ask myself: Was I going to drop out of school? Was I going to let the engineering program beat me down? Or, was I going to make the decisions I need to make to get through that program? I had to constantly ask myself, what am I trying to accomplish? Ultimately, I decided that running track and a bunch of other things I was doing were not as important as my goal to graduate from the University of Rochester with an engineering degree."

After quitting the track team, Talley says he eliminated other distractions and focused on his studies. "I didn't cut off having friends or watching TV occasionally," he shares. "I had to ask, why am I in college really? I had to put my focus on that. The track team was taking a lot of time, so it had to go away. I could not go away on spring break. I could not leave. My engineering friends and I had to stay and study. So I couldn't do road trips."

Talley completed the program with guidance and support from his chair. "Three years later when he passed me my diploma, he said, 'Tim I'm sorry I didn't believe in you as much as you believed in yourself."

Talley later earned an MBA from Duke University and worked in various capacities at Kodak, Nestle', and New Era Caps. He leads U-Lace No-Tie sneaker laces (www.U-Lace.com) and won an investment from billionaire Mark Cuban on the Shark Tank business television show.

You can come back from a bad semester or year. Look within yourself and explore what kept you from performing at a higher level. Also, be willing to ask program administrators, tutors, and fellow students for help.

CHAPTER 4
From B.A. to Payday: Majors and Consequences

There are many factors to consider when determining your academic major. Emerging professionals know that a college degree is not what it used to be. They know that having just any university diploma is not an automatic ticket to a middle-class life. That's why they purposely select majors and career paths that will help them make a profitable return on their educational investment. Yes, difference makers understand that their education is an investment that should yield dividends they can use to finance their future, donate to causes, issues, and organizations they care about, and create their desired quality of life. Conduct research and explore the opportunities.

Anthony Carnevale, Ph.D., economist and director of the Georgetown University Center on Education and the Workforce (GUCED) maintains:

> "So many people are frustrated with the fact that they go to college and nothing seems to happen. They don't appear to do much better (economically) than people that didn't go to college. Being in the wrong fields can cause you to make much less money. Among bachelor's degrees, the most well paid major is petroleum engineering. On average you will earn about $130,000 a year. If you get a degree in elementary education or psychology, you will make about $30,000 a year or less. In the end, it comes down to what you're after."

This assessment may provoke a few questions:

- How do I pick a major?
- Should I base my major on what I like?

- Should it be based on my passion?
- Should it be based on my future earning potential?
- Should it be a mixture of all of the above?

Sonny Arre grappled with these questions a few years ago. Arre's life is filled with many ironies. He saw his Haitian-immigrant parents rise from one of Miami's poorest and crime-riddled neighborhoods and move to one of its more affluent communities. He attended excellent schools and earned spots in academic magnet and gifted programs. Despite having family support, great schools, and proven academic potential, Arre quit high school.

> "I was getting into so much trouble during high school. I was into girls, clothes, and being a class clown. I was thrown out of William H. Turner Tech High School in Miami. I later went to another local high school, an adult education center, and a school in another city, and got kicked out of all of them. So, I quit school. My 'gifted' mind had me thinking I was smarter than everybody and I didn't need to waste my time with school. I was thinking about starting a business and making money like Bill Gates. I later earned my GED before my fellow classmates graduated from high school."

After receiving his diploma, Arre moved to Tallahassee with some of his childhood friends. During that time, he failed in a business venture, had a few run-ins with the law, and flunked out of Tallahassee Community College. A catastrophic event led him to begin changing his hard-partying ways.

> "While I was in Tallahassee, one of my best friends was shot to death. And, I had to tell his mother what happened. That event and her reaction helped me take my faith in God more seriously. I was sitting on the couch one day, and this commercial for a tech school came on. I signed up for the X-Ray technology program and started two months later. I have not looked back since. I did my

research and saw that I would only make about $40,000 a year. I could make $50,000 or more if I specialized in a modality. I then looked at what type of house I wanted to live in, what kind of car I wanted to drive, and some other things, and it just didn't add up.

Once I started doing clinical rotations, it became apparent to me that I could be more than an x-ray technician. I was always interested in some form of healthcare or medicine because I believe that saving lives is the best thing you can do. I liked the idea of becoming a doctor because I would learn skills that would help me save lives and it would pay enough salary so I could live how I wanted to live."

The former high school dropout understood that remaining on a lower-paying career path would not help him achieve his goals. Arre decided to pursue additional training that would help him upgrade his skill set and create a higher quality of life. Arre successfully graduated from both Miami Dade College and Florida International University (FIU) with the highest honors.

After graduation, Arre was accepted into FIU's Herbert Wertheim College of Medicine. He hopes to practice emergency medicine after graduating from medical school and completing a residency. Making the switch to emergency medicine helped him upgrade from an average x-ray technician salary of $40,000 to a projected average emergency medicine physician salary of more than $320,000.

"People should not be afraid to think about the money. I tell my mentees to go on CareerBuilder and see how many jobs are available in their majors and find out what the salaries are," offers Arre. He says he wants to use his disposable income to further his deceased father's business ventures and his Glory Over Defeat (GOD) non-profit organization that ministers and provides services in the USA and Haiti. "I want to build a legacy for my family and my community."

Sometimes students may come from underprivileged backgrounds or have a strong desire to make a social impact for a cause or community. Dr. Price Cobbs, who along with Judith L. Turnock wrote *Cracking the Corporate Code: From Survival to Mastery* (Executive Leadership Council), counsels students to have an open mind when considering a career path.

"Broaden your palate," advises Dr. Cobbs, founding CEO of Pacific Management Systems, a corporate diversity management consultant firm. "Expand the canvas you are looking at and the kinds of things you want to do. I hear so many students who say, 'I want to give back to my community.' That is great, but many times you can give back more to your community if you get a higher-paying profession that allows you to build wealth, thereby you can help your community. So much of being empowered is about developing the resources to be empowered. You have to create and see a bigger picture."

Explore your options with these additional resources.

- Shatkin, Laurence and The Editors at JIST. *10 Best College Majors for Your* Personality (JIST Works)
- Fogg, Neeta, Harrington, Paul, Harrington, Thomas, and Shatkin, Laurence. *College Majors Handbook with Real Career Paths and Payoffs Third Edition* (JIST Works)
- *Encyclopedia of Careers and Vocational Guidance, 17th Edition, 6-Volume Set* (Ferguson Publishing Company).

***

Not All Degrees Are Created Equal

Millions of students use student loans to pay for school. Understanding your future loan payments, your desired quality of life, and the expected salary for your major and skill set could go a long way in helping you determine your best path forward. It is important to have a career that allows you to repay your student loans ten years after you graduate (See: Paid in Full: The Price of Education).

Dr. Carnevale explains some majors are more profitable than others over the long-term. "We've known for a while that all degrees are not created equal. Your major has a large effect on your ability to get a job and work your way up a career ladder.

There are many reasons to go to college, but nearly 80 percent of college students look for a college education to give them access to a solid career that will give them a living wage."

Dr. Carnevale and colleagues Jeff Strohl, Ph.D., research director at Georgetown University Center on Education and the Workforce, and Michelle Melton, M.S., MSFS, an associate fellow at the Center for Strategic and International Studies, authored "What's It Worth? The Economic Value of College Majors." The 182-page report uses census and other economic data to analyze wages for 137 college majors. Among other insights, the report highlights the most popular college majors and the economic output of undergraduate majors.

"It is true that on average, going to college will improve your earnings substantially above a high school diploma. There is a big 'but' that comes after that," Dr. Carnevale cautions. "While that has been true since the 1980s, what has been even truer is that it all depends on your college major."

Dr. Carnevale admits that sexism, racism, and a lack of influential contacts, can also have an adverse impact on a person's earning potential (See: Networking Success for College Students). "The only explanation for that (behavior) is discrimination. The extent of that is something that is much debated. The fact that it exists is not debatable."

Dr. Carnevale offers a solution, saying, "In the end, the one way you can beat that is by choice of major." He says choosing the right career path can help decrease wealth and income disparities.

Among other findings, "What's It Worth? The Economic Value of College," highlights analysis of the most and least popular majors (See: Table 3); undergraduate majors with the highest and lowest median earnings (See: Table 4 and Table 5); and the undergraduate majors with the highest and lowest employment rates (See: Table 6 and Table 7).

Your education and career choices have a serious impact on your lifetime earning potential and your ability to accomplish your social justice, family, and economic goals. It is hard to support the issues, causes, and institutions you care about if you do not have disposable income. Creating wealth also helps you enjoy a greater sense of freedom. Consider the following questions as you make your personal, educational, and professional decisions:

- What is the expected utility and relevance of the profession?
- What is the average income and compensation range for people of that profession?
- Does the income justify the cost of schooling and training?
- How much debt will you incur through schooling?
- How much risk is there regarding income?
- Is there a steady, predetermined income?

TOP 10 MOST POPULAR MAJORS	TOP 10 LEAST POPULAR MAJORS
Business Management	Precision Production & Industrial Arts
General Business	Military Technologies
Accounting	Nuclear Engineering
Nursing	Soil Science
Psychology	Geosciences
Elementary Education	Pharmacology
Marketing and Marketing Research	Educational Administration and Supervision
General Education	Astronomy and Astrophysics
English Language and Literature	Geological and Geophysical Engineering
Communications	School Student Counseling

Table 3. SOURCE: "What's It Worth? The Economic Value of College"

Boyce Watkins, Ph.D., an economist and author of *Everything You Ever Wanted to Know About College* (Blue Boy Publishing Company), says understanding the salaries and employment rates of your intended career path can also guide your choice of a major. Dr. Watkins recalled choosing an alternative major before entering his doctoral studies at the Fisher College of Business at The Ohio State University.

> "I thought about getting a doctorate in mathematics, but then I did some research and saw that many people with math doctorates weren't even making $100,000, or they were unemployed. My mentor recommended I consider getting my Ph.D. in finance. After doing the research, I realized that many people with this degree earned six-figures or more right after they graduated. I also noticed that I took many of the same courses that the math doctorates took, so I was able to get mathematics along with a more marketable skill set."

Like Dr. Watkins, you may be able to find a major that is similar to your passion and skill sets, yet offers you the opportunity to meet your financial goals. "What's It Worth? The Economic Value of College" also displays the undergraduate majors with the highest and lowest median earning potential (See: Table 4 and Table 5). You can benefit from learning the employment rates of your prospective major. You may not want to invest your education in a dying industry. Dr. Carnevale notes, "It is very important to understand that if you are pursuing a particular major, you want to learn who the people are that completed that major and how they are doing professionally and financially."

The U.S. Bureau of Labor Statistics (www.bls.gov) and O*NET OnLine (www.onetonline.org) are great resources that will help you research anticipated job and sector growth. "What's It Worth? The Economic Value of College" also identifies the majors that have the highest and lowest employment rates (Table 6 and Table 7). Pursuing a career in a sector that has a higher unemployment rate than the national unemployment rate might not be a wise choice.

Make sure you consider the financial consequences and job outlook for prospective majors. It is also helpful to ask people in your network or graduates from your program their perspective on the job market and salaries.

TOP 10 UNDERGRADUATE MAJORS WITH HIGHEST MEDIAN EARNINGS	
Petroleum Engineering	$120,000
Pharmacy, Pharmaceutical Sciences and Administration	$105,000
Mathematics and Computer Science	$98,000
Aerospace Engineering	$87,000
Chemical Engineering	$86,000
Electrical Engineering	$85,000
Naval Architecture and Marine Engineering	$82,000
Mechanical Engineering	$80,000
Metallurgical Engineering	$80,000
Mining and Mineral Engineering	$80,000

Table 4. SOURCE: "What's It Worth? The Economic Value of College"

Noted economist Julianne Malveaux, Ph.D., encourages students to consider other ways they can make money with their skill set. She urges students to:

> "Always have a plan B and multiple income streams. For example, you may want to be a teacher, but is there something else you can do with it? Can you be a teacher who does programming on the side, or one who takes on a private client or two? What happens if indeed the school system you want to work in doesn't work out? Do

you also have something else, like maybe a counseling certificate? Have you developed relationships with people in the teacher's unions and others who can turn you on to substitute teaching?

TOP 10 UNDERGRADUATE MAJORS WITH LOWEST MEDIAN EARNINGS

Health and Medical Preparatory Programs	$40,000
Communication Disorders Sciences and Service	$40,000
Drama and Theater Arts	$40,000
Studio Arts	$40,000
Visual and Performing Arts	$40,000
Social Work	$39,000
Theology and Religious Vocations	$38,000
Human Services and Community Organization	$38,000
Early Childhood Education	$36,000
Counseling Psychology	$29,000

Table 5. SOURCE: "What's It Worth? The Economic Value of College"

I really admire the young people who want to do business. They are not only looking at perhaps getting a job in a corporation; they have side hustles, which might involve things like building webpages for people and other things that folks of my generation have a challenge doing.

I tell folks to think about multiple income streams. All this seems very definitive, but none of it is. Life changes and circumstances change. Always think about your alternatives and having more than one income stream. If this does not happen, how are you going to bring money in? If you lose your job, what are you going to do?"

TOP 10 MAJORS WITH HIGHEST EMPLOYMENT RATES	
Geological and Geophysical Engineering	100%
Military Technologies	100%
Pharmacology	100%
School Student Counseling	100%
Medical Assisting Services	99%
Metallurgical Engineering	99%
Treatment Therapy Professions	99%
Agricultural Economics	98%
Agriculture Production and Management	98%
Atmospheric Sciences and Meteorology	98%

Table 6. SOURCE: "What's It Worth? The Economic Value of College"

Dr. Malveaux is a doctoral graduate of the Massachusetts Institute of Technology and founder of Economic Education, LLC. Find out more at www.JulianneMalveaux.com. Take responsibility to craft a first-class curriculum that prepares you for 21st-century opportunities. You can accomplish that by:

1. Researching the colleges with the top five academic programs in your major.
2. Comparing and contrasting those programs' required courses to your required curriculum.
3. Working with your adviser to build a curriculum that is consistent with what the country's best programs in your major are currently doing.
4. Consider minoring in subjects that are desired by the dominant, high paying industries.

TOP 10 MAJORS WITH HIGHEST UNEMPLOYMENT RATES	
Social Psychology	16%
Nuclear Engineering	11%
Educational Administration and Supervision	11%
Biomedical Engineering	11%
Linguistics and Comparative Language and Literature	10%
Mathematics and Computer Sciences	10%
United States History	10%
Court Reporting	10%
Counseling Psychology	10%
Studio Arts	9%

Table 7. SOURCE: "What's It Worth? The Economic Value of College"

CHAPTER 5
COLLEGE: AN ENTREPRENEURIAL LAUNCHING PAD

> 66 *"Too many of us gravitate to the idea that we must get educated to work for someone else instead of getting educated to own a business."*
> —**Boyce Watkins, Ph.D.**, Economist, Author 99

What do companies like Facebook, Dell Computers, Microsoft, and Google have in common? They were all founded by college students. "I wish I had been more open to entrepreneurship while I was in college," recalls Omar Goff, who enjoys a career at a Fortune 500 company. "I viewed my educational experience as grooming me for the corporate world."

In *The Millionaire Next Door: The Surprising Secrets of America's Wealthy* (Rosetta Books), authors Thomas J. Stanley, Ph.D. and William D. Danko, Ph.D. reveal that two-thirds of America's millionaires are either self-employed or own a small business. "I've learned a lot and live a good life," Goff continues. "But, the real opportunity for wealth comes from ownership. I feel like I missed a huge opportunity by not seriously working with my peers to create entrepreneurial possibilities."

Dr. Boyce Watkins, scholar, and owner of www.48HourBusinessSchool.com, encourages students to think about graduating from college and into business ownership.

Dr. Watkins, author of *It Takes a Village to Raise the Bar*, maintains, "Jay-Z is not wealthy because he's a rapper. He is a businessman. Oprah Winfrey is not a multi-billionaire because she was a talk show host. She is a multi-billionaire because she owned her television show. Own something! That's how you build wealth in America."

There are at least two schools of thought concerning college students and business ownership. The first encourages students to start a business while they are in school or immediately after they graduate.

"More young people should consider testing their entrepreneurial skills in the college setting, where there are lower risks, and leverage the opportunity to build meaningful relationships that will unlock great potential in the future," Goff suggests.

Acclaimed entrepreneur Randal Pinkett, Ph.D., started his first venture as a third-year engineering student at Rutgers University. "In the early '90s, we didn't have a campus music store. So, students had to leave the school to buy music," recalls Dr. Pinkett, a Rhodes Scholar and author of *Campus CEO: The Student Entrepreneur's Guide to Launching a Multimillion-Dollar Business* (Kaplan Business). "I found out how to get compact discs from a wholesaler and had them delivered to me overnight. I bought the CDs for $7. I would sell them for $10-$15 and deliver them to the client's dorm."

Dr. Pinkett, who in 2005 won "The Apprentice" business competition television reality series, says opening a successful enterprise begins with seeing a problem and creating an opportunity.

"Entrepreneurs see and capitalize on opportunities that others don't see," adds Dr. Pinkett, chairman and CEO of The BCT Partners, a multimillion-dollar management, technology, and policy consulting services firm. Dr. Pinkett encourages college students to have confidence in themselves and recognize their power.

"Young people are trendsetters that impact everybody else. If you think about it, Facebook, Hip-Hop, and Google were all spawned by young people. Now, the world uses all of those products," he offers. "Embrace your student status. Embrace your culture, and create the things that the people you are looking at need."

Dr. Pinkett concludes, "You must have a passion for your business because people are attracted to passionate people. It's important to know your strengths and weaknesses because you can partner with or hire someone to do the things you are not good at."

Dante Lee traded his cap and gown for a shingle that read, "CEO of Diversity City Media, Inc." Lee, who has been self-employed since completing Bowie State University's Computer Science program in just three years, says it also takes character to build a sustainable business.

"You are young only once. That is when you are most creative and most energetic. Use that time to build your business," says Lee, an awarding-winning entrepreneur. "It takes determination, goal setting, and having the right priorities to become successful."

Lee says all business owners must be able to adapt to their customers' needs. He warns, "There is always something to learn and things are always evolving. You must adapt or you will die."

Lee first started BlackHeadlines.com in hopes of making money with an online newspaper catered to a Black audience. "Then, I received a lot of calls and e-mails from people asking me if my company could help them get their stories in newspapers around the country," he recollects.

Lee cashed in on this demand by completely changing his business model from posting stories online to creating BlackPR.com, an affordable service that sends press releases to media outlets nationwide. His company, which generates hundreds of thousands of dollars each year, has interests in websites (www.ScholarshipsOnline.org), e-book publishing (www.UrbanEBooks.com), tourism (www.thePhilippines.com), and marketing services (www.BlackPR.com).

Although the idea of being a business owner can seem ideal and possibly glamorous, in reality, most businesses fail within two years. Under the best conditions, only 33 percent of firms survive 10 years or more, per the U.S. Labor Department. There are generally four challenges that complicate business success:

- Not having enough money to support the business.
- Not having enough useful and influential relationships to help the business grow.

- Lack of awareness and inexperience with industry trends.
- Lack of an established reputation or highly specialized knowledge.

Additionally, "One of the biggest things that stop people from achieving business success is procrastination and fear of failure," Lee informs. "I talk to many people. They have great ideas. I see them a year or two later, and they have not done anything with their ideas. Then I see people that try something, it didn't work, and they quit working. Sure, I've had ideas that worked and others that didn't. The difference for me is that I implement and keep trying to produce results from my ideas."

***

The Entrepreneurial Learning Curve

The second school of thought regarding students who aspire for business ownership is to encourage pupils to find the best career opportunity that will prepare them for commercial success. IACM recommends the 3L Approach to Successful Entrepreneurship: Learn, Leverage, and Launch.

LEARN: ON-THE-JOB TRAINING

You can increase your chances of business success by working for a leading company and learning the best practices in your industry, before venturing out on your own.

"Make your mistakes on somebody else's dime," reveals George Fraser, who, before launching FraserNet, Inc., worked for a myriad of companies including Procter and Gamble, Ford Motor Companies, and United Way of Cleveland. "I learned so much while working at Procter and Gamble. I spent millions of dollars of their money learning marketing skills and how to manage a business."

This approach was also helpful for Aubrey J. Ross, DVM, co-owner of Cy-Fair Animal Hospital, with Diarra D. Blue, DVM, and Michael Lavigne III, DVM. The animal-loving trio also stars in "The Vet Life" reality television series aired on Animal Planet.

After graduating from Tuskegee University's College of Veterinary Medicine, the veterinarians worked for established animal medicine practices and hospitals in Las Vegas.

> "While in Las Vegas, we were able to experience fast-paced medicine, exciting cases, and perform a high volume of surgeries," Dr. Ross shares. "I always knew I wanted my own practice. I decided to branch out and learn all I could while I was there."

The Houston, Texas native broadened his clinical skills by building relationships with colleagues who had exotic, avian, and other medical experiences. Eventually, Dr. Ross earned the lead veterinarian post at a local franchise of a Mars, Inc.-owned national animal hospital. He recalls:

> "Later I went to Banfield Pet Hospital, a large corporation. They do things differently from general practitioners. While there I learned the business aspects of veterinary medicine. I was responsible for profit and loss statements. Those experiences prepared me to manage my practice in the Houston-area."

LEVERAGE: CASHING IN ON YOUR KNOWLEDGE

While working for someone else, gather all the business intelligence you can. After you have proven to your industry, professional peers, customers, and companies that you are highly competent, you are now ready to cash in on your knowledge and experience.

While the Labor Department says the average veterinarian earns $88,490 yearly, these doctors earn more money by using the information they learned as employees.

"While working in Las Vegas, we saw the amount of money you can truly make as a veterinarian if you handle things in a certain way," Dr. Blue says. "We saw they made money by having late hours, offering emergency services, off-site vaccinations, and things of that nature. We mimic some of those things in our practice."

LAUNCH: OPEN FOR BUSINESS

The partners launched their holding company, Animalscopic, which earns income by owning Cy-Fair Animal Hospital, managing Conroe Animal Adoption Center, and starring in Animal Planet's "The Vet Life" reality television series. The co-owners created and are enjoying their version of the American dream.

"Being an owner allows us to earn more capital than being an associate veterinarian ever would have," remarks Dr. Blue.

Dr. Ross adds: "Every day I thank God for allowing me to live my dream. A lot of people are intelligent, but so many people fall short of their goals because they lack confidence or resources. I get to wake up and go to my own animal hospital every day."

The group hopes to franchise animal hospitals across the country.

IACM offers several resources to propel your journey toward creating your version of the American dream:

BUSINESS COMPETITIONS

- **2016 U.Pitch Competition & Showcase**
  Award Amount: Multiple awards totaling $75,000
  Website: www.futurefounders.com/startup/upitch

- **Ford HBCU Business Classic Competition**
  Award Amount: $5,000
  Website: www.fordblueovalnetwork.org/programs

- **Graves Undergraduate Business Plan Competition**
  Award Amount: First Place: $5,000; Second Place: $3,000; Third place: $2,000
  Website: www.andersoncei.utk.edu

- **Miller Lite Tap the Future® Business Plan Competition**
  Award Amount: Multiple awards totaling $200,000
  Website: www.mltapthefuture.com

BUSINESS RESOURCES

- **AMERICA'S SBDC**: A nationwide network of Small Business Development Centers (SBDC) offering free small business assistance. Many of the centers are connected to universities. Visit www.AmericasSBDC.org for more information.

- **CAMPUS RESOURCES**: Many college campuses offer numerous resources for aspiring student business owners. Some of those resources include incubator spaces, business and subject matter experts (professors and staff members), computer and technology lab access, and research reference materials. Employees in the business school, the Office of Student Affairs, and the campus library are valuable resources as well.

- **MINORITY BUSINESS DEVELOPMENT AGENCY (MBDA)**: A U.S. Department of Commerce agency aimed at helping minority entrepreneurs. Discover more at www.MBDA.gov.

- **SCORE ASSOCIATION:** A nonprofit association of volunteer business counselors offering free sessions throughout the country. Log on to www.SCORE.org, for more information.

- **UNITED STATE SMALL BUSINESS ADMINISTRATION (SBA)**: Among other services, SBA offers training, funding assistance and support to small business owners. Find more information at www.SBA.gov.

BUSINESS BOOKS

- Beech, Wendy. *Black Enterprise Guide to Starting Your Own Business* (Wiley)

- John, Daymond and Paisner, Daniel. *The Power of Broke: How Empty Pockets, a Tight Budget, and a Hunger for Success Can Become Your Greatest Competitive Advantage* (Crown Business)

- Johnson, John H. and Bennett, Jr., Lerone. *Succeeding Against the Odds: The Autobiography of a Great American Businessman* (Johnson Publishing Company, Inc.)

- Lewis, Reginald F. and Walker, Blair S. *Why Should White Guys Have All the Fun?: How Reginald Lewis Created a Billion-Dollar Business Empire* (Wiley)

- Pinkett, Randal. *Campus CEO: The Student Entrepreneur's Guide to Launching a Multimillion-Dollar Business* (Kaplan Business)

- Ries, Eris. *The Lean Startup: How Today's Entrepreneurs Use Continuous Innovation to Create Radically Successful Businesses* (Crown Business)

CHAPTER 6
DOLLARS AND CENTS: FINANCIAL LITERACY

> 66 *"Financial literacy is having a basic understanding of how to make financial decisions in a way that is beneficial for the individual."*
> — **Kevin Cohee, J.D.,** Chairman, CEO,
> OneUnited Bank 99

The U.S. Federal Reserve's "Economic Well-Being of U.S. Households" report points out that nearly 80 million American adults are struggling financially or just getting by. It also reveals that almost half of them could not cover a $400 emergency expense with their savings. You deserve a better life than that. Use your college experience to learn financial habits and principles that will help you create a sustainable life, support your family, and donate to important issues and organizations.

Negative financial peer pressure is one of the biggest obstacles to prosperity. Many people experience pressure to buy meals, clothes, and entertainment to fit in or impress the crowd. These practices — especially when they are financed with debt — can ruin your financial future and have long-term consequences. Robert L. Johnson, MPA, became America's first Black billionaire when he sold Black Entertainment Television (BET) to multimedia conglomerate Viacom for $2.34 billion.

Johnson says avoiding financial peer pressure helped him build a 10-figure fortune. "I think about one thing, savings and postponing conspicuous consumption," says Johnson, a graduate of Princeton University's prestigious Woodrow Wilson School of Public and International Affairs. "Conspicuous consumption is buying things because they are there, buying things because companies advertise them to you, and buying things you don't need just because you think that's the way to be hip, cool, or to be in with the crowd."

Johnson shared that creating wealth allowed him to donate to the National Museum of African American History and Culture, the Congressional Black Caucus Foundation, and support economic development on the continent of Africa. The founder of the NBA's Charlotte Bobcats (*now* Hornets) franchise says it is important to use positive financial peer pressure by connecting with people that apply healthy financial habits.

Michael Lee-Chin, Canada's first Black billionaire, agrees:

> "No man is an island. Make sure you use other people's brains. We need to surround ourselves with people who have the knowledge, experience, and a track record of creating wealth. They can be an investment adviser who has a sound philosophy, a tax consultant, an insurance adviser, or people who have experience and are focused on creating wealth."

Lee-Chin owns a diverse portfolio of businesses in Canada and the Caribbean. Among them are Portland Holdings, Inc., the National Commercial Bank of Jamaica, Advantage General Insurance Company, CVM Communications Group, among other interests. Lee-Chin has been generous with his time and money. He donated millions of dollars to Northern Caribbean University, Royal Ontario Museum, the University of Toronto, and other groups. The Jamaica-born philanthropist says having a goal is the first step to creating financial success.

"If you aim at nothing you will hit it with amazing accuracy," asserts Lee-Chin, who did not inherit his wealth. "Articulating your goal is the first principle of financial success."

Lee-Chin, an engineering graduate of McMaster University, shared three principles that helped him build a reported $3.26 billion net worth:

- **PLAN AND ATTACK:** "You have to have a goal. Most people do not have goals. Once you have a goal, have a plan of attack to achieve your goal."

- **SAVE 10-PERCENT OF YOUR INCOME:** "I save at least 10 percent of everything I earn. I set it aside and compound it. So, a part of everything I earn is mine to keep."
- **INVEST WISELY:** "Every wealthy person has built wealth by investing in strong, high-quality businesses, and holding them for the long-term."

***

Budgeting 101: Developing Your Plan of Attack

Your financial habits will create your future. "The real thing is saving and investing for your future and your kids' future," Johnson urges. "Also, you have to figure out ways to reduce unnecessary spending. Those are the most important things."

Tiffany "The Budgetnista" Aliché, an award-winning financial empowerment teacher, says your spending habits reveal your true desires.

"How you spend your money is based on your values," she explains. "Look at your bank statements, withdrawals, and payments. Then ask, is this who I am? For example, you can't say you like to read or save money if all you see are charges from fast food restaurants and the mall. That shows me your values are based on eating out and dressing nicely, not reading."

Aliché, who wrote, *The One Week Budget: Learn to Create Your Money Management System in 7 Days or Less!* (CreateSpace), encourages students to write down all expenses and create a budget. She says you don't have to have a job to create a budget. She notes:

> "Students still get and spend money, so they must have a plan for it. We have been fooled into thinking of budgeting as something that limits us. I grew up with the perception that a budget frees you. I don't see my budget as limiting. My budget says yes I can go on vacation or yes I can get my hair done. I make my budget tell me yes.
> You are in charge! You have to manipulate the numbers to make your budget tell you yes. You may have to cut

something to do the thing you want to do. I look for what I can reduce to get my yes.

If you have a physical budget that you can see, you can manipulate your money and plan for long-term goals. Sometimes, my budget says you can't do that activity now, but you can do it six months later if you save."

Aliché encourages students to adopt a financially empowering mindset:

"Money is like a hammer. A hammer is a tool that can be used to build a house. That same hammer can be used to destroy a house. Who decides what that hammer does? The person who is holding it. The same thing applies to money. Money can build up your life, but you can also use money to destroy your life. Who decides what your money will do? Money doesn't do what it wants. You decide. Once you realize that you are in control, there is no limit to what you and your money can do."

She concludes with a thought-provoking challenge, "We always hear people ask what do you want to be when you grow up? The ultimate question should be, how do you want to live?"

After pondering how you want to live, use short-term and long-term investments to accomplish your goals.

***

Managing Your Present: Short-Term Investments

Short-term investments are the best vehicles to save your day-to-day money and emergency funds because they are safe and federally insured. Kevin Cohee, J.D., president and CEO of One United Bank, recommends you make companies compete for your dollars. "One of the keys to making the best financial decisions is knowing how to get the best deal when buying things," says Cohee, a graduate of the Harvard University

College of Law. "Most people don't recognize that when you put money in a bank, you are buying a financial product. You are purchasing a savings or checking account. It's no different from buying a car."

Cohee recommends using all of the available resources to help identify the best products at the lowest price.

"It's common sense to look for products with the most benefit and the least costs. It's the underpinning of being a financially literate person," he continues. "The less money you have, the more important it is for you to be financially literate. You have to make good financial decisions because you don't have resources to throw away."

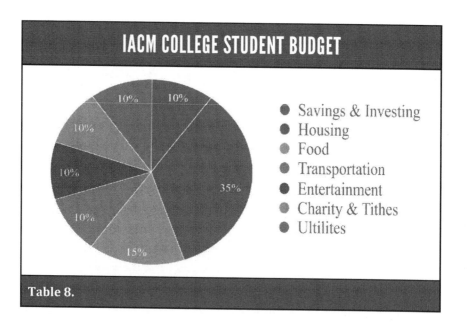

IACM COLLEGE STUDENT BUDGET

- Savings & Investing
- Housing
- Food
- Transportation
- Entertainment
- Charity & Tithes
- Ultilites

Table 8.

Having a basic understanding of short-term financial products can help you when developing a plan to establish a stable economic foundation:

- **INTEREST AND CREDIT RATES:** Use BankRate.com and NerdWallet.com to find banks offering the highest interest rates and which credit cards offer the best perks and lowest interest rates.

- **SAVINGS ACCOUNTS:** Savings accounts are liquid deposit-based accounts that allow you to save and withdraw money when you are ready. You usually earn a nominal interest rate. Savings accounts are best for storing money for emergencies and short-term goals.

- **CHECKING ACCOUNTS:** Checking accounts are also liquid accounts that allow you to manage your expenses. Many financial institutions offer free checking accounts. Users make transactions via check writing, Automatic Teller Machine (ATM) cards, withdrawals, and deposits. Checking accounts are best used for day-to-day expenses.

- **MONEY MARKET ACCOUNTS:** A Money Market Account (MMA) is a liquid account similar to a savings account. They offer higher interests with a catch. There is usually a minimum balance requirement and limited monthly withdrawals. Some MMAs allow you to write a limited amount of checks each month. Verify the MMA terms with your financial institution.

- **CERTIFICATES OF DEPOSIT (CD):** Purchasing a CD gives your financial institution a loan with your promise not to withdraw that loan for an agreed period. CDs offer guaranteed interest. Time periods range from 3-6 months, and 1-5 year intervals. Withdrawing from your loan before time requires you to give up some of your earned interest.

Financial coach Ash Exantus, also known as Ash Cash, recommends pursuing long-term investments along with your short-term investments. "I think students should consider starting to invest in securities while they are in college because the one thing you can't get back is time," Cash notes. "They can benefit from the compound interest. If they invest from ages 18-25 years old, they could also make a lot of money.

***

Managing Your Future: Long-Term Investments

" *"It's not how much money you make, but how much money you keep, how hard it works for you, and how many generations you keep it for."*
— **Robert Kiyosaki,** best-selling author,
Rich Dad, Poor Dad (Warner Books) "

Since the founding of the Board of Brokers of Philadelphia in 1790, Americans have invested in securities (stocks and bonds) to create wealth. Wealth is money that grows over time and eventually works for you. The more wealth you have, the more freedom you can enjoy. Securities offer many advantages including compound interest.

COMPOUND INTEREST

Albert Einstein called compound interest, "the most powerful force in the world." Economists describe compound interest as interest earned on the starting amount plus the growing interest over a period of time. For example, if you put a $1,000 one-time investment in an index fund, after five years you would have earned $1,402.55, assuming you earn 7 percent interest.

Let's take it a step further. If you keep the $1,000 in the index fund, plus add $25 every pay period, after five years you would have earned $ 9,401.83, while earning the same 7 percent interest.

Use the compound interest calculator at MoneyChimp.com to make calculations. No firm can guarantee future investment performance.

Many affordable long-term investment vehicles can help you build wealth. They include:

- **STOCKS:** Stocks represent a portion of ownership in a company. If you own one share of a company that has a million shares, you own one-millionth of that company.

You can purchase stock shares with a stockbroker or online brokerages like Scottrade and Charles Schwab. Mobile apps like Stash, Acorn, and Robin Hood allow you to invest in small amounts at comparatively low fees.

- **BONDS:** A bond is an asset that lets you loan a company or government money for an agreed time period, usually at a fixed rate. Businesses and governments use bond funds to pay for projects and activities. You may have to forfeit some interest if you withdraw funds before the agreed period. Find out more information about bonds at www.investinginbonds.com and U.S. Savings Bonds at www.TreasuryDirect.gov.

- **MUTUAL FUNDS:** Many investors use mutual funds as their first investments. In fact, the U.S. Securities Exchange Commission notes 1-in-3 Americans use them to build wealth. Mellody Hobson, president of Ariel Investments, describes mutual funds as, "a basket of securities that include stocks and bonds." Shares represent partial ownership in every asset in which your fund invests. Your money gets pooled with other investors' money to purchase stocks, bonds, and other assets. The company earns money when those assets increase in value. You make money by selling shares for more than you bought them for. Some funds offer quarterly payouts called dividends.

The Princeton alumna says mutual funds offer three benefits like professional guidance, diversification, and low entry costs.

- **PROFESSIONAL GUIDANCE:** "With mutual funds you're not sitting at home trying to figure which stock to buy, betting your whole future on something. You have trained professionals doing that for you."

- **DIVERSIFICATION:** "If one stock goes up one day and another stock goes down, they balance each other out.

You don't have all of your eggs in one basket. They are spread across a portfolio of companies."

- **Low Entry Costs:** "Companies like Ariel allow you to invest for as little as $50 per month. The great thing is that in one month you may be investing when the stock market is up a lot. Another month, you may be investing when the stock market is down a lot. Overall, during the long-term, you average a better price by consistently and methodically investing."

If you invested $50 per month for 10 years and earned 8 percent interest, you would earn $9,387.29. After twenty years it's $29,653.75, and thirty years it's $73,407.52. Imagine if you invest more (See: Table 8). You can purchase mutual funds shares individually, online, or with a broker. You can monitor your shares' value by typing the fund's ticker symbol online with services like Yahoo! Finance or looking it up in a newspaper's business section. Most companies allow you to withdraw funds via check or wire transfer to a connected bank account.

***

Creating Excellent Credit

Understanding your credit score and how credit works is a major component of financial empowerment. Savvy students know that having a bad credit score can make their lives more expensive and challenging. Ash Cash wrote *What the FICO: 12 Steps to Repairing Your Credit* (1Brick) to empower readers with steps they can take to build or get their credit in a great space. Cash explains:

"I define credit as the ability for someone to trust you. The someone, in this case, is a creditor – the credit lenders, banks, financial leaders, etc. Instead of judging you off your appearance or statements, they look at your credit score to determine whether you are trustworthy enough to lend money. Your score also determines the amount that creditors think you can afford to pay back. Your credit score allows you to gain the trust you need and allows lenders to see your history of keeping your promises."

Financial literacy and education erases intimidation. "The biggest trap is lack of knowledge. Too many college students dive head first into these credit opportunities without thinking about the consequences," mentions Cash, who also created the IAmAshCash.com financial empowerment platform. "Knowledge is power! It is important to understand how credit works and realize credit is not free money. You have to pay it back. Knowing those things will help us protect our credit."

Low credit scores make life expensive because when lenders see you as a risk, they charge you more. It can also make it difficult to rent a car or book a hotel room.

"Car, homeowners, and renters' insurance companies can charge you more fees because your credit score says that you are risky," Cash cautions. "There are even cases where utility companies are charging people more money because of low credit scores."

Fair Isaac Corporation (FICO) is a data analytics company that measures your credit risk and history. Lenders report your payment behavior to three major credit reporting agencies: Equifax, TransUnion, and Experian. The scores range from 300 through 850. The higher your score, the more creditworthy you are (See: Table 9).

"Consumers have many different credit scores, but 90 percent of lenders look at your FICO score," informs Cash, a longtime banking executive.

Cash says there is no excuse for not understanding your credit. The financial coach provided a few answers to frequently asked questions concerning credit literacy:

- **HOW DO I BUILD CREDIT?** "If you don't have any credit, you will not activate a score. This is not a bad rating. It just means you haven't activated a score."

CREDIT SCORE RANGES

CLASS	RANGE	CLASS	RANGE
Excellent	800-850	Fair	650-699
Very Good	750-799	Poor	600-649
Good	700-749	Very Bad	300-599

Table 9. SOURCE: Fair Isaac Corporation (FICO)

- **HOW DO THEY CALCULATE MY CREDIT SCORE?** "Your credit score is broken down into five categories. I like to call it the 35-30-15-10-10, to help people better understand the five areas. They are your payment history, outstanding debts, credit history, number of accounts, and type of credit used." (See: Table 10).

- **WHAT IMPROVES OR HURTS MY SCORE?** "The biggest chunk that determines your credit score is your payment history and usage ratio. That accounts for 65 percent of your score. If you pay your bills on time and keep your credit balances low — 30 percent of your credit limit or less — you are on your way to building excellent credit. If you have a $1,000 credit limit, make sure you spend less than $300. Anything above that has an adverse impact on your score. Use credit cards for emergencies. Don't use them for everyday purposes."

- **WHERE CAN I GET A CREDIT REPORT?** By law, you are entitled to a free credit report each year. Visit https://www.annualcreditreport.com/ to view your report.

- **WHERE CAN I GET MY CREDIT SCORE?** Many financial institutions are now offering complimentary access to your credit score. You can also secure your credit scores from reporting agencies including TransUnion, Experian, and Equifax. CreditKarma.com provides free access to credit scores.

Additionally, it is important to protect your identification and credit. It is not a good idea to share your credit card or social security information with other people. The overwhelming majority of identity theft victims were attacked by people they knew or to whom they were related.

FIVE CREDIT SCORE CATEGORIES

PERCENTAGE	BREAKDOWN
35 Percent	**Payment History.** Do you pay your bills or fines on time?
30 Percent	**Outstanding Debts.** This is based on the amount you owe each of your creditors, and how that compares with the total credit available to you or the total loan amount you took out. If you're maxing out your credit cards, your score may suffer.
15 Percent	**Credit History.** How long have you had credit accounts? How long have you used them? The fewer and older the accounts, the better (assuming you've paid on time).
10 Percent	**Number of Accounts.** How many accounts have you recently opened? How many do you already have? Are you letting too many creditors search your credit? Are you trying to get debt that exceeds your ability to pay it back?
10 Percent	**Type of Credit Used.** What kind of debt do you have (e.g., mortgages, credit cards, revolving debt)? Do you pay off the balance every month, or do you pay the minimum?

Table 10.

IACM COLLEGE STUDENT MONEY CHALLENGES

GOALS	BENEFITS
Find Financial Role Models	Billionaire Robert L. Johnson challenges you to find people who apply the financial habits you want to have.
Pay Yourself First	Billionaire Michael Lee-Chin encourages you to save at least 10 percent of everything you earn. Then, put it in an online savings account.
911 Fund	Build a $3,000 emergency fund (minimum) for life's ups-and-downs. It could also help fund moving, internship expenses, and other necessities during and after school.
Invest $50 in Securities	Benefit from compound interest by investing $50 per month in mutual funds or other securities.
Pay Bills on Time	Remember, 35 percent of your credit score is based on paying bills on time.

Table 11.

CHAPTER 7
PAID IN FULL: THE PRICE OF EDUCATION

Among other definitions, the American Economic Association describes economics as, "the study of scarcity, the study of how people use resources or the study of decision-making." It will take significant resources (money, relationships, effort, and time) to pay for your education and living expenses while in college. Your job is to become aware of all resources that can help you pay your costs promptly. You must also accomplish your goal in the most economical way, meaning paying for your expenses by incurring no debt or as little debt as possible. Other than paying out of your pocket, this chapter will help you understand three ways to pay for college: student loans, need-based grants, and uniformed service obligations.

***

Life with Debt: Student Loans

For the first time in American history student loan debt has surpassed credit card debt. The Federal Reserve reports Americans have accrued $1.4 trillion in unpaid education debt versus $779 billion in credit card debt. The Institute for College Access & Success reveals that 69 percent of public and nonprofit college graduates had an average debt of roughly $30,000.

Dr. Julianne Malveaux, a former president of Bennett College, offers this consideration, "Students have to be very careful with loans. Students should do research on salaries they may earn in their first jobs. Whatever amount that is, that is the maximum amount of loans they should get, only if they have to." For example, if your projected starting salary were $40,000, using Dr. Malveaux's logic, you would only get loans totaling $40,000.

"Ideally, they want to repay student loans within 10 years after graduation," Dr. Malveaux explains. "They can also use income-based repayment programs to repay some loans as well." Using 10 percent of your income enables most borrowers to repay their loans within a decade of graduating without dramatically altering their quality of life. Remember, it is best to live like a college student once.

The biggest advantages of federal loans are that they tend to have lower borrowing rates and Income-Based Repayment programs that allow you to repay loans based on a portion of your income.

The federal government offers subsidized and unsubsidized loans designed as low-interest financial assistance to help students pay for their education:

- **DIRECT SUBSIDIZED LOANS:** are for undergraduate students who have financial need. The U.S. Department of Education pays loan interest while you are in school. You have a six-month grace period after you leave school before repayment.

- **DIRECT UNSUBSIDIZED LOANS:** are for undergraduate and graduate students regardless of financial need. Your school determines the loan amount. Interest accumulates during school and grace periods.

- **DIRECT PLUS LOANS:** are Department of Education loans with interest offered to parents of dependent undergraduate students.

- **FEDERAL PERKINS LOANS:** are low-interest federal student loans for undergraduate and graduate students who have exceptional financial need. The total lifetime limit may not exceed $27,500 for undergraduates and $60,000 for graduate students (including amounts borrowed as an undergraduate).

You can find out more information about loans at www.StudentAid.Ed.gov. You can also secure private loans through financial institutions and other sources. Terms and responsibilities vary depending on the lender.

Meharry's Dr. Farmer-Dixon encourages students to consider long-term consequences when managing financial aid. "Federal financial aid has its limit. You cannot exceed a certain amount of dollars," Dr. Farmer-Dixon notes. "If students are serious about going to graduate and professional schools, they cannot use all of their aid for their undergraduate education."

The dental school dean explained that because the government has maximum loan limits, students must understand the impact this funding limit can have on their academic pursuits. Graduate and professional schools are more expensive and more academically challenging than their undergraduate counterparts. Running out of the cheaper federally supported loans or using a substantial portion of your aid on a bachelor's degree can increase your graduate school costs.

"The average indebtedness of our students is between $250,000 and $300,000. That's a scary number," Dr. Farmer-Dixon reveals. "Many of our students have to get the more expensive private loans that require co-signers."

Finding co-signers can prove difficult if they have poor credit or do not have income and assets to secure six-figure loans. Co-signers are responsible for the payments if the student defaults.

***

Free Money: Grants and Scholarships

You can minimize your loan exposure by maximizing grant and scholarship opportunities. The federal student aid website StudentAid.Ed.gov describes grants and scholarships as "gift aid" because they are free money — financial aid that does not have to be repaid. Pell Grants are the most widely used need-based federal grants. In certain scenarios, grantors may require that a portion or all of the grant funds be repaid if you do not fulfill grant requirements.

Grants are often need-based, while scholarships are usually merit-based. They can come from governments, schools, foundations, businesses, and other entities. You can find out more about grants and scholarships at:

- www.StudentAid.Ed.gov
- Your state's and the federal Department of Education
- Your financial aid or scholarship adviser
- By researching scholarship books or your favorite search engine
- Creating a Google Alert for "college grants" and "college scholarships"
- *Scholarships, Fellowships, and Loans* (Gale, Cengage Learning), a comprehensive directory of education-related financial aid available

In some cases, grants and scholarships are not enough to finance college. Many schools offer work-study programs to help offset expenses. The student financial aid office administers work-study opportunities.

"I always tell students to seek jobs that 'pay' them to be a student," says Delatorro L. McNeal, II. "These jobs include being an assistant in the library, laboratory, or a departmental office. It is not laborious work. It allows you to build relationships, and you can usually study on the job."

***

Cashing In: The Billion Dollar Scholarship Sweepstakes

Each year students apply for billions of dollars in scholarships. If you want a piece of the multi-billion-dollar pie, UNCF's Dr. Michael Lomax recommends creating attractive applications that feature personal narratives.

"Students must understand the importance of telling their story and making their case effectively," notes Dr. Lomax, who has led the multi-million-dollar scholarship fund and college student support organization for more than a decade. "The most important skill is for students to be able to tell a compelling story."

Ryan Davis, M.Ed., is a former senior program manager for the multi-billion dollar Gates Millennium Scholars Program (www.GMSP.org). The Bill & Melinda Gates Foundation funded the $1.6 billion initiative aimed at providing outstanding ethnic minority students the opportunity to complete an undergraduate education in any discipline interest.

"Make sure you are authentic in your responses and give the scholarship interviewer a piece of you," adds Davis, now serving as director of Assessment and Educational Programs at Purdue University. "Don't write what you think the reviewer wants to hear. Also, avoid generic responses. It does not tell reviewers anything about you as an individual. If the reader is reviewing hundreds of applications, a generic response won't stand out, so they will refer to your academics only."

Davis, a doctoral student at the University of Indiana-Bloomington, offers tips to help you cash in on the scholarship sweepstakes:

- **UNDERSTAND AND OBEY GUIDELINES:** "Follow the instructions. If you don't, you will be disqualified."

- **BUILD RELATIONSHIPS EARLY:** "You want to get strong recommendation letters. Not all counselors and teachers are equal. Develop relationships very early. Strong recommendations will showcase your strengths and demonstrate that you are a good fit for the opportunity. If your desired person is not enthusiastic about writing a recommendation, you have to move on to someone else. Your job is to do whatever it takes to get a strong letter of recommendation, so build that foundation early."

- **DEVELOP STRONG LEADERSHIP SKILLS:** "Articulate the ways you have led, not just from a position standpoint. Communicate the way you changed something for the better. What was the outcome of your work? How does that leadership role relate to your long-term interests and goals? Making those connections allows you to come off more powerful on the application. If you say you are president and didn't say what you did, then reviewers will wonder what you contributed in your role."

- **SERVE YOUR COMMUNITY:** "Community service is a portion of leadership. I remember talking to a GMSP alumnus. This alum interacted with Bill Gates. The alumni told him how grateful they were for the scholarship. Bill Gates said, 'Great, but what are you going to do and what are you doing now to give back?' He was most concerned about the reproduction of service. Giving back to your communities is important. Service is huge."

- **ASK FOR HELP WITH ESSAYS:** "Put great effort into writing your essays. Have someone look at it. Then rewrite it again. I think those things make you competitive as a scholarship applicant."

- **PERFORM WITH EXCELLENCE:** "In terms of reporting your grades and your transcript, the better you do – especially in core courses like math and science – the more competitive you are. If you do well in honors courses that is even better."

- **START EARLY, SUBMIT EARLY:** "We have thousands of people who miss the deadline because they waited until the last minute. There is a lot of unclaimed scholarship money because either people don't apply or they applied too late."

When applying for scholarships, Dr. Lomax encourages students to, "Show up, fill out the forms, and keep at it. If you do it often enough you are going to get something!"

If scholarships and grants do not pay all of your student expenses, you can consider going to a cheaper school or asking your "Uncle Sam" for support.

***

Uncle Sam Can Help: Federal Assistance

John Pierre, J.D., chancellor of the Southern University Law Center, credits part of his educational and professional success to the U.S. Army. Pierre says his scholarship and experiences as a U.S. Army Reserve Officers Training Corp (ROTC) cadet prepared him "for the professional rigors of life."

"The benefits of getting the ROTC scholarship meant that I didn't have to borrow any money to go to college. I also got a monthly stipend and free books," recalls Pierre, a graduate of Southern University.

The former accountant and tax attorney says it also helped him earn three degrees debt-free.

"It transformed how I approached college. I didn't have to work or do odd jobs," Pierre recalls. "I really got a chance to spend a lot of time focusing on being a college student. It made all the difference in the world and allowed me to be a strong candidate for graduate school and eventually law school."

Captain Todd Lacy, MBA, spent the latter part of his military career extending the same opportunity to cadets in the Naval ROTC program at Savannah State University (SSU).

"We afford an opportunity for young people to be a part of a profession that gives them real world leadership experience," says Lacy, a professor of Naval Science, and program commander at SSU.

Like its fellow military counterparts, NROTC offers partial and full scholarships, book and living stipends. Students are required to serve paid summer military duty. Each support level has different requirements.

"We are looking for academically and physically qualified students," Lacy shares. "They must also have integrity, aptitude, great communication skills, and character."

He admits the program is rigorous:

"Our midshipmen have to be here at 5:30 a.m. Then, we have them running and doing various physical activities (kettle bell, swimming, calisthenics, etc.) during the week. We do physical training (PT) three days a week. Marine cadets have PT five days a week and the midshipmen who are struggling also have it five days a week.

When you graduate, you become an ensign in the Navy or a second lieutenant in the Marines. They get a leadership experience that you can get in only a few places. We are one of the only places you can go where you are guaranteed a job."

All federal uniformed services offer college and scholarship programs. The scholarships have service requirements for graduates. They also have programs to help you repay student loans if you remain enlisted for an agreed period. Additional information can be found at:

COMBATANT UNIFORMED SERVICES

- **U.S. Army:** www.GoArmy.com/ROTC
- **U.S. Air Force:** www.AirForce.com/Education
- **U.S. Navy:** www.Navy.com/Joining/College-Options
- **U.S. Marine Corps:** www.Marines.com
- **U.S. Coast Guard:** www.GoCoastGuard.com

NON-COMBATANT UNIFORMED SERVICES

- **National Oceanic and Atmospheric Administration Commissioned Corps (NOAA Corps):** www.OMAO.NOAA.gov/Learn/
- **U.S. Public Health Service Commissioned Corps (PHSCC):** www.USPHS.gov/Student/

There are also numerous employers and nonprofits that offer loan repayment benefits.

CHAPTER 8

MIND, BODY, AND SOUL: MENTAL, PHYSICAL, AND SPIRITUAL ENRICHMENT FOR THE COLLEGE SOUL

66 *"The foundation of success in life is good health. That is the substratum fortune. It is also the basis of happiness. A person cannot accumulate a fortune very well when he is sick."*
— **P.T. Barnum**, Co-founder,
Ringling Bros. and Barnum & Bailey Circus 99

Mind right. Body right. It may sound cliché, but it is hard to become successful if you are not mentally, physically, and spiritually healthy. "I do not separate mental health from overall health," says Curley L. Bonds, M.D., professor and chair of the Department of Psychiatry at Charles R. Drew University of Medicine and Science. "If you want to function and succeed in life you must have a great sense of wellness."

Your health is your wealth. The National Wellness Institute defines wellness as a healthy balance of the mind, body, and spirit that results in overall wellbeing. Use your time in college to develop the habits needed to build lifelong health in every area of your life.

***

Mental Health Impacts College Students, Too

Do you feel worthless? Are you constantly unhappy? Are past mistakes holding you back? Do you dislike activities you used to enjoy? If you answered yes to any of these questions, you might have a treatable mental illness.

Cinnamon Key, MSW seemed like a typical student at Barry University nearly 10 years ago. Despite being friendly and outgoing, Key just could not shake her constant sadness.

She recollects: "I was just doing. I was just going and just being. I would go somewhere and not thoroughly enjoy myself. I would be around my friends and still feel lonely. I communicated and still felt misunderstood. I did not feel comfortable or complete no matter what I did."

Key was one of the more than 7 million American college students who, per the Association for University and College Counseling Center Directors (AUCCD), suffer from a form of depression or mental illness. Dr. Bonds describes mental illness as, "any illness that troubles your thinking, concentration, mood or behavior."

"Ultimately, having great mental health means living life to the fullest without any thought, mood, or anxiety problems getting in the way of anything you want to achieve," he informs.

The Substance Abuse Mental Health Services Administration notes college students are more likely to suffer mental illnesses than older adults.

"Young adults are sometimes at increased risk because many of these illnesses first appear during the 18-21 age range," Dr. Bonds adds. "During this time, there is a lot of brain and growth development, hormonal changes, and students are away from the safety of the home. They also have to create their own rules and patterns. This can cause some students to get off track."

Mental health challenges can also cause some students' grades to suffer. They can even decrease a pupil's drive and ambitions. Retired psychiatrist Dr. Price Cobbs, says young scholars must "push themselves to aspire," despite their challenges. He explains that your journey to healing begins by recognizing your issues.

"The healthiest people are the people who can acknowledge their situation, then examine the reasons why they have an issue. Once you acknowledge it you must figure out what you are going to do about it," encourages Dr. Cobbs, who, along with fellow psychiatrist William H. Grier, M.D., co-authored *Black Rage: Two Black Psychiatrists Reveal the Full Dimensions of the*

Inner Conflicts and the Desperation of Black Life in the United States (Basic Books).

AUCCD information states students with mental illnesses can also experience poor sleep, poor physical health, higher dropout rates, and increased substance abuse risks. Key experienced something far worst during her last undergraduate semester.

"I was juggling so much at that time," Key shares. "My father had two different kinds of cancer and I was trying to manage my academic responsibilities. I was overwhelmed. I got the idea to end my life while driving down a winding road. I decided to go fast, jump the curb, and crash into a tree. I floored the pedal, but my car wouldn't accelerate."

This was Key's fourth failed suicide attempt. It helped her understand that she was unhappy. She wanted to change and confessed that she, "Didn't know what to do." A friend encouraged her to talk to someone at school.

"I approached my program director seeking help to get deadline extensions from my professors," she remembers. "After I told her about my suicide attempt. She wanted to suspend me to help me get better."

The thought of disappointing her parents with news of a delayed graduation only added stress. After hearing Key's concern, the program director agreed not to suspend her on one condition – that she visit the counseling center weekly and bring back proof.

Like many students, Key had not considered using the counseling center until she was forced to. National Alliance on Mental Illness research reveals that 40 percent (approximately 8 million) of college students do not seek help for their mental challenges.

Bernadette Smith, Ed.D., director of the University Counseling Center (UCC) at Texas Southern University (TSU) in Houston, helps students overcome mental challenges through behavioral or talk therapy and counseling. "Time is going to pass regardless of what you do," Dr. Smith offers. "With mental health, we tend to ignore the symptoms and issues. Ignoring them allows them to pile up. You can learn how to deal with them now, or you can allow them to hinder your ability to accomplish your goals well into your 30s."

Dr. Smith says you do not have to suffer alone. TSU's UCC offers individual and group counseling. It can help students manage depression, anxiety, and emotional challenges among other concerns. It is common for students to seek counselors for situations ranging from grief, stress, and even before taking major tests. Despite these student-fee covered resources, Dr. Smith says some students do not use them because of false information.

**

Counseling is Confidential

Dr. Smith explained it is against the law for therapists or counselors to tell anyone which students are using counseling services unless they intend to hurt themselves or others. She adds that services, "won't become a part of your student record."

"We all have ups and downs in life. Counseling teaches you how to celebrate the ups and manage the down times," she explains. She adds therapy is not a sign of weakness.

For Key, it was a means of self-empowerment. "Counseling helps you uncover the cause of the mental challenge you're dealing with at the time and gives you the tools to deal with it," Key emphasizes. "As college students, we think somebody is going to make you okay. Nobody can make you okay. You can use counseling to build skills to handle things when you are slipping into a sad state."

In therapy, Key said she discovered a significant cause of her depression. "I learned that I was doing it to myself because my parents supported me and bragged about me. I put so much pressure on myself to be perfect. I was trying to live up to too many expectations," she divulges. "My counselor asked me, 'Did your parents say they expected you to be perfect?' I said no."

For Dr. Smith, this is the aim of counseling. She shares, "We tailor each session to help students develop a framework for success. The goal is to help students manage whatever good or bad situation may come up in their future."

Dr. Smith encourages students to consider five steps toward mental wellness:

- **TRY IT**: "Visit the counseling center and schedule a counseling session. What's the worst thing that could happen if you go?

- **CREATE A JOURNAL**: "Journaling gives you an outlet to write out your concerns and create an action plan."

- **MAKE TIME FOR YOURSELF DAILY**: "Take a little time each day to do something enjoyable for yourself."

- **ENJOY THE PRESENT**: "Be aware of the feelings you are experiencing at the time and enjoy them."

- **UNDERSTAND YOUR TRIGGER POINTS**: "Let us help you identify your trigger points and develop a plan to cope and manage the symptoms."

If you go through counseling or therapy and find that your mental health challenges persist, you have another option. "Generally, a patient and their therapist may consult a psychiatrist if a patient's progress is taking longer than expected," explains Dr. Bonds, who is also the medical director of Didi Hirsch Mental Health Services in Los Angeles.

A psychiatrist is a physician that treats mental diseases with medication. "Mental illness is a disease," Bonds informs. "Sometimes there are certain chemicals and cells in your brain that might not be working properly. Psychiatric medications can help improve or correct certain chemical imbalances and cell activity in your brain."

Dr. Bonds does not recommend patients use medication by itself. He encourages therapy combined with medication for best outcomes.

Key agrees. "Medicine can help you feel better so you can use the coping mechanisms and tools you learn in therapy," says

Key, who is now a clinical mental health professional and owns Jamila Wellness, LLC, a mental health treatment firm.

Additionally, Dr. Bonds prescribes healthy nutrition, sleep, and regular exercise for increased overall wellness.

Vanessa Blowe, M.D., staff physician at the Spartan Health Center at Norfolk State University in Norfolk, Virginia, adds, "Your mind and body are connected. You must take your health seriously if you want to be sharp and perform at a high level."

***

Student Health Centers are Valuable

"Students must take responsibility for their health," warns Dr. Blowe. "As a doctor, it is sad when I see people succumb from an illness that could have been prevented if the patient acted sooner."

On many campuses, student health center costs are included within tuition fees. Spartan Health Center treats illnesses as well as minor injuries. The center offers preventive care, health education, sexually transmitted disease screenings, vaccinations and contraceptives.

"Most colleges require students to get certain vaccinations before admission. In addition to those, I highly recommend students get Tetanus boosters, flu shots, meningitis, and HPV (Human Papilloma Virus) vaccinations," she prescribes.

These centers typically employ licensed healthcare professionals to provide medical services.

"We offer care for students who may have a long-term illness like allergies, diabetes, or hypertension," she continues. "We are also able to work with students' primary care physicians to treat issues and refer them to specialists if necessary. We are here to answer any student's health questions or concerns."

Dr. Blowe recommends students get physicals, health screenings (blood pressure, cholesterol, diabetes, etc.), and understand their family's medical history. She says this information can help save their lives.

"Understanding your family's history with diseases can help us develop a plan to help you avoid certain risk factors and preventable diseases," she adds.

She also encourages students to, "Find a physical activity or exercise that you can carry throughout your life so that you can be prepared to manage your stress and overall health."

***

Fitness Centers Keep Students Strong

Anthony Daniels, M.S., director of Intramurals and Recreational Sports at Prairie View A&M University (PVAMU) agrees with Dr. Blowe. "Being active is the start to a great quality of life," he remarks. "Research says active students perform better in school. If you look better, you feel better, and naturally, you perform better."

The American College of Health Association reports that 1-in-3 college students are obese. "Centers for Disease Control and Prevention (CDC) suggest we exercise at least three times per week for at least 60 minutes for overall health," Daniels advises. "You want to include a warm up period, 60 minutes of activity, and then a cool down period."

PVAMU's recreation center boasts a 93,000 square foot facility with three gymnasiums, an indoor suspended track, an Olympic-size swimming pool, a 28-foot climbing wall, and plenty cardiovascular equipment and free weights. It also offers body and fitness screenings all designed to help students attain peak fitness.

Marquies Brown recalls walking a short distance on campus and feeling as if he had run a marathon. His heavy breathing concerned him. "I am a father, and I wanted to be here for my child," says Brown, a kinesiology and mass communications major.

The San Diego, California native made up his mind that he would no longer carry his 353-pound frame. He committed himself to including more physical activity into his daily routine.

"I decided to walk every day. I parked my car and rode my bike to school. I would use the stairs instead of the elevator," he reveals. "I also exercise in the recreation center five times a week. It was convenient and helped me get closer to my goal."

After 15 months, Brown now sports a 239-pound figure. In addition to already melting 114-pounds, he aims to lose 50 more pounds.

"Losing weight and enjoying a healthy lifestyle opened me up more. I find myself being more willing to network and connect with people," he adds. Brown attributes his successful weight loss to patience and consistency.

Some students like Leticia Bustamante, a PVAMU graduate student, use campus fitness facilities to gain weight. "People used to think I was anorexic," Bustamante explains. "I came here with a different mindset." She did not like her 98-pound build. With exercise, she sculpted a physique she is now proud of.

"I actually came here (recreation center) to gain weight, gain muscle, and look fit," recalls Bustamante, who now sports a five-foot, seven-inch, chiseled 142 pound frame.

"I am no longer embarrassed by how I look. I love my body now. I have the body of an 18-year-old because I am so fit," she beams. "Even though I gained more than 40 pounds, I've lost fat and have about 17 percent body fat. Gaining the weight really boosted my confidence."

Daniels says he wishes more students would experience a level of fitness and confidence in school and life. "We want them to continue to be active and participate in sports long after their college careers," he continues.

Daniels offers a four-part solution to help students avoid the colloquial "Freshman 15":

- **CONSULT YOUR DOCTOR:** "Ask your doctor if you are healthy enough to exercise."

- **GET INSTRUCTION:** "Sure, you can exercise on your own, but one of the benefits of the recreation center is that we can teach you how to do it right. You will learn how to stretch and properly use the equipment."

- **START WHERE YOU ARE:** "Just start moving! Do not be ashamed if you have to start with walking. Walking is a lifetime sport. It makes a difference."

- **KEEP EXERCISING:** "You have to be consistent if you want results. You must also have a good attitude."

***

Best Dietary Habits for the College Student

Fitness and nutrition go hand in hand. No matter how hard you work out in the gym, bad dietary habits will decrease your results. It does not help that most campuses have buffet style dining halls or that students are prone to late night eating. If you are eating poorly, one university-based dietician guarantees your body will pay the price.

"Research shows that if you eat healthy food, in the long run, your body will respond with higher energy and better health," explains Joycelyn M. Peterson, Dr.PH, MPH, and RDN, chairwoman of the Nutrition and Dietetics Department at Oakwood University. "If you eat improperly you are going to have an unhealthy body. You also increase risk factors for diseases."

Dr. Peterson says excellent nutrition gives students an edge in school and life. She continues, "Eating healthfully helps your body, cells, and brain work better and clearer. It increases your memory and performance. It also slows down the process of disease occurring in the body."

She counts missing breakfast as the biggest nutritional mistake among undergraduates. "We've discovered that students who don't eat breakfast have a lower attention span," she says. "Unfortunately, too many students skip breakfast or eat junk food in the morning."

Dr. Peterson encourages students to eat healthier food and to create a plan for eating unhealthy food. "We keep it positive.

We never tell a student not to eat something," she says. "If you feel like you are punishing yourself, you won't be successful in reaching your dietary goals."

The internationally acclaimed nutritionist says these four strategies will help you create nutritional success:

- **PLAN YOUR FATTY FOODS:** "If you like pizza or fried chicken, try to eat it only once or twice a week."

- **LOAD UP ON FRUITS AND VEGETABLES:** "Eat at least two fruits and three vegetables every day. Try to eat the real fruit, not the juice, which has more sugar. Apples are better than apple juice."

- **DRINK WATER:** "A lot of people forget about this nutrient called water. Your body needs at least eight to 10 glasses of water daily."

- **ADD FIBER:** "Fiber is very important for energy and elimination. Eat high-fiber foods daily like whole grains (brown rice, whole wheat pasta, and whole grain bread). You want to eat vegetables as close to their natural form as possible."

It may be helpful to limit your time in dining halls to a maximum of 45 minutes and avoid eating after a certain evening time. It is also imperative to get rest. Many doctors and medical groups recommend young adults get eight hours of sleep for a healthy quality of life.

***

Spiritual Strength for College Students

The body has been described as the temple of your soul. Spiritual health is an equal piece of your holistic wellness. What would you do if you still had nightmares after seven years of sexual abuse from your stepfather? What if you believed your mother passively stood by while it happened? What would you do if you had to travel nearly 40 miles, across two counties via public transit, to attend college? What would you do if you have to manage all those elements while you were pregnant and had to transport three toddler-aged children? If you were Deandra Poythress, MSW, you might be overwhelmed. However, Poythress says she was determined not to let her circumstances get the best of her.

"College was not easy because of the struggles I've endured. I also didn't have transportation and could not afford to pay for daycare," Poythress admits. "I had to carry my children with me to school because my husband was the only one working."

Poythress says juggling her personal and academic responsibilities while overcoming traumatic experiences was challenging.

"Most of the time, I would just numb myself, numb my emotions, numb my feelings, and just be numb to everything. I would disassociate myself and I was very anti-social," she remembers.

"I would get to school at 6 a.m. and start praying before I got to class," she recollects. "I would sit out front of the school building and just sing, read my bible, and pray." She says doing so helped her manage her life more effectively.

"After building up myself spiritually, I found completing school assignments, managing my household, and other things less overwhelming. I realized that I did not have to rest in my own strength. I could have faith that God strengthened me to do whatever he assigned me to do. Spirituality brought me through all of my obstacles."

Poythress graduated magna cum laude from Florida Memorial University in 2012, and earned a master's degree in Mental Health Counseling from Barry University in 2015. She chose a career in mental health counseling to help children overcome challenges and obstacles they may face. The wife and mother of four has forgiven her mother. She attributes her success to, "a praying and faithful husband and the power of God."

The Honorable Benjamin Carson, M.D., says his spiritual strength increased as his faith matured. Dr. Carson used this strength to overcome a poor academic start in inner city Detroit and graduate from Yale University and the University of Michigan Medical School.

"My key to success is first and foremost; you must have principles that guide your life. You can't be blown by every wind that comes by," says Dr. Carson, a first-generation college graduate who currently serves as U.S. Housing and Urban Development Secretary. "A steady anchor for me has been my faith in God, God's word, and God's principles. That takes care of almost everything else that you do because everything is constrained by those principles."

Payne Theological Seminary President Michael Brown, Ph.D., made it his life's work to help people enhance their spiritual foundation to overcome whatever obstacles life puts in their way.

"I stand in awe of people who come through horrific circumstances and yet are able to achieve," says Dr. Brown, author of *The Lord's Prayer and God's Vision for the World: Finding Your Purpose through Prayer* (Engaging Media). "It is so easy to shut down and think that the present time is all there is. It is our development of our spiritual capacity that allows us to go beyond a painful present and have hope for the future."

He defines spiritual capacity as, "An unlimited power that makes us human. This power transcends time, yet empowers us in the present moment."

Dr. Brown says increasing your soul force offers many benefits and enables you to overcome your past, your limitations, and insecurities. He advises that spiritual growth is key to unlocking your human potential.

"If you only view your education as a means to a goal, you will miss the opportunity to learn what it means to be human," he submits. "Don't come to college just to learn how to acquire things. In college, you have the opportunity to actually develop into the person you want to be. You can learn to give yourself to something higher than yourself."

The respected theologian offers a six-step approach to building a strong spiritual foundation:

- **GET GROUNDED AND CONNECTED:** "It's easy to get disconnected from any sense of community outside of your campus. Being isolated can have a negative impact. Find a religious community in the area that you can be a part of."

- **EMBRACE COMMUNITY:** "Your community becomes people you can pray with and they often become some of your biggest supporters."

- **MAKE TIME TO MEDITATE:** "During college, I would consistently schedule myself to take a bath every evening to decompress, let go of the day, and reconnect to my spiritual source."

- **PRAY:** "Let go of the cares of today and avoid the anxieties and worries of things that might not have happened yet. Give them to a power that is higher than yourself."

- **REMEMBER, YOU ARE CHOSEN:** "God chose us despite our shortcomings. God is still for us. God does not change God's mind. There is not a "No" on earth that can contradict the Divine's "Yes" on your life."

- **NEVER GIVE UP:** "I made so many mistakes. I never imagined I would be nearly 50 years old. Our people have overcome so many terrible things by the power of a merciful God who loved and strengthened them. Keep going forward."

IACM MIND, BODY, AND SOUL ACTION ITEMS	
FOCUS	**WELLNESS ACTION**
Mind	Take your mental health seriously! Please consider scheduling and attending at least one counseling session. Allow the counselor to help you develop a plan to manage stress, anxiety, or the necessary adjustments that come with life and college.
Body	Make sure you get your required vaccines and any health screenings offered by your campus health center. Find an exercise or physical activity you enjoy then exercise at least three times per week. Go to your campus recreation center and try various exercises. Stay hydrated by drinking eight glasses of water daily. Eat two fruit and three vegetable servings daily. Try hard to get an average of eight hours of sleep each night.
Soul	Identify a faith community, forgive yourself for past mistakes, and schedule time to meditate and decompress daily.
Table 12.	

CHAPTER 9
TO LOVE OR NOT TO LOVE: REALITIES IN COLLEGE RELATIONSHIPS

> " *"No boy is cute enough to keep you from getting an education. If I had worried about who liked me and who thought I was cute when I was your age, I wouldn't be married to the president of the United States."*
> —**Michelle Obama**, J.D., First Lady of the United States (2009-2017) "

When Magda Demerritt, MSW, stepped on the campus of Florida International University she was thrilled to be in a new environment. For the first time in her life, she was away from the confines of her strict parents and ready to dive deep into the fullness of her college experience. Now, she had power – power to choose her classes, the power to choose her activities, and like millions of other college students she had the power to create a love life without much judgment or input from her parents, something she was not able to do in her ultra-conservative Haitian home.

"Coming from a history of abuse myself, I defined myself by my relationships. I spent my entire college experience making attempts to attach myself to people and as a result did not make a good name for myself," she recalls. "I performed well in my studies, but I still made mistakes that continue to impact me and my relationship with my husband, even today."

Demerritt, a licensed clinical social worker pursuing a doctorate in social work, says craving romantic connections is common among undergraduates, especially first-year students.

"New college students, especially those living on campus, are in a vulnerable state because they are detached from home," she reveals. "Once we disconnect from the home, we are instinctively looking to attach ourselves to something or someone. We are in search of our new community."

Unfortunately, this quest can leave a student susceptible to engaging in unhealthy romantic relationships. While love can be a beautiful, energizing, and exciting experience, it takes grace and wisdom to balance it and keep it in its proper place. If you are forced to make a decision between your education and a relationship, please choose your studies. One longtime education executive recommends students give more energy to achieving their educational and professional goals versus falling in love.

"It is fine and appropriate for students to engage in social interactions and experiences. Students are here to learn what they may like or prefer from a relationship perspective, but not to necessarily get married or to have an incredible relationship," suggests President Abdullah of Virginia State University. "I think students invest too much time and energy into relationship management and trying to change themselves to meet someone else's expectations. This, hands down, is the No. 1 complication for college students!"

***

Creating Standards and Boundaries for Healthy Relationships

Changing yourself to meet your love interest's expectations is neither helpful nor suggested. On average, most college relationships last about three months. The Independent Women's Forum notes 63 percent (roughly 7.4 million) of college women hope to meet their spouse in college. Conversely, a Facebook Data Sciences study found that only 30 percent (nearly 3.5 million) accomplish that goal. With such a low success rate (3 out of 10), you must ask yourself, am I willing to pay a permanent price for a likely temporary situation?

"You need to be focused on the love of your life, which is yourself," declares Alfred Edmond, Jr., co-author with Zara Green, of *Loving in the Grown Zone: A No-Nonsense Guide to Making Healthy Decisions in the Quest for Loving, Romantic*

Relationships of Honor, Esteem, and Respect (Balboa Press). "You are complete, whole, and capable as a single person. There is nothing magical about being a couple."

After four divorces and multiple self-described ineffective relationships between them, Edmond and Green created GrownZone.com, a self-love and relationship empowerment platform. They regularly comment in national media and conferences about relationships and their brand of grown self-love.

Edmond and Green observed that many people do a lot to prepare themselves for professional success through coaching and mentoring. Few people, however, make the same effort to learn the skills necessary to love themselves and their love interests successfully. The two built their platform to help people prepare themselves for relationship success. In a recent Grown Zone newsletter, Edmond summarized that a successful life is based on healthy professional, personal, and relationship habits. He added, anyone could make a fortune, but if you have poor relationship skills you will lose it in divorce court.

The couple says if you are not comfortable with yourself, then you are not ready for a relationship. "Your most important relationship – even after you are in a relationship with someone – is your relationship with yourself," informs Edmond, who earned a bachelor's degree in studio art from Rutgers University-New Brunswick. "Your relationship with yourself is the foundation for all other relationships."

Edmond and Green say your maturity level is tied to you accepting responsibility for every part of your life.

"Being grown is about taking ownership and responsibility for protecting yourself," they proclaim, "and not counting on your parents, church, professors, or anyone else to protect you. You have to protect yourself. When all is said and done, it is your own decision making that puts you at risk."

Loving yourself means advancing your best interests. Since you are responsible for protecting yourself, you do not have to submit to anyone or any setting that puts you in danger.

"You have a right and an obligation to say, 'I own myself, I own my body, I own my money, I own my heart, and I own my personal space,'" Edmond asserts, "and it's your responsibility to make self-loving decisions that will protect those things, regardless of your gender. You cannot say, oh that person said they loved me, so I expected them to protect me. No! It's on you to protect yourself."

The couple says being "horny," "catching feelings," or "being in love," are not excuses for making poor relationship decisions that can result in financial hardship, emotional despair, a sexually transmitted disease, or worse.

"Do not allow anyone to objectify your body for their purposes," adds Green, a psychology and mass communications graduate of Xavier University of Louisiana. "If you decide to engage in something (sexually), do it for your own pleasure, not for someone's enjoyment."

In *Living in the Grown Zone,* Edmond and Green encourage people to limit access to their body, money, homes, and hearts, while evaluating whether a potential suitor is a healthy relationship partner or fit (See: Table 13).

"These things bind you to other people," he informs. "You should not surrender these things when you first start a relationship."

Edmond says protecting and limiting access to your body, money, house, and heart, makes it easier to separate from an unhealthy or unfit relationship. He warns, "If you risk these four things, you are risking the foundations of your life."

They advise students to mature into grown living by developing the courage and discipline to adopt and use healthy habits. They say the only way to do this is by setting standards for what you require and want in your life and boundaries for the things you do not want in your life.

"Different things will be healthy for you at different times in your life," adds Green. "As you grow and mature, your standards and boundaries will evolve. They will get better, tighter, and stronger. You have the final say on what is healthy for you!"

After protecting yourself, it is important to communicate with yourself and your love interest honestly.

BOUNDARIES FOR SAFE AND HEALTHY RELATIONSHIPS

AREAS	POSITION	DANGERS	EXAMPLES
BODY	Don't allow your body to be used for other people's purposes. If you decide to engage in something, do it for your own pleasure.	Bodily health, ability to have kids, and having kids before you are ready.	Uncomfortable sexual positions, performing sex acts in public or with others, or being pressured to have sex when you do not want to.
MONEY	Don't give your mate access to your personal information or your PIN number. Everything is fine when you're in love, but they can use that information against you when times are bad. Don't spend a whole lot of money that you do not have financing a relationship.	Credit ruin, financial ruin, identity theft, and potential adverse impact on jobs that require good credit scores.	Co-signing for apartments, cars, or anything else; sharing credit and identification information; using credit cards to pay for someone else's purchase; borrowing or loaning large amounts of money.
HOME	Don't allow someone to violate your personal space or have free access to your home or dorm room.	You may start feeling uncomfortable in your home, which adds stress and anxiety.	Giving a person free access to your living space, even when you are not there.
HEART	When you give access to your body, your money, and your home, you will have an emotional attachment. Save yourself the heartache and the emotional baggage by restricting access to these areas.	The emotional and psychological consequences of any and all the above mentioned actions.	Using love as an excuse to make decisions without thinking them through. Virtually agreeing to your partner's request without considering the consequences in the name of love.

Table 13. SOURCE: Edmond, Jr., Alfred, and Green, Zara .*Loving in the Grown Zone* (Balboa Press), www.GrownZone.com

***

*Honesty is the Best Policy: Be Honest with
Yourself and Your Significant Other*

"College students have to decide the level of seriousness they want at this stage in their lives," says Demerritt, who also owns Wonderful Counselor LLC, a mental health counseling services firm. "You have to decide what kind of relationship you are looking for. Are you looking for a potential spouse, or are you going to be casually social while you are working on your degree?"

Demerritt says making those decisions in advance will help you focus on what is important to you. "This way, you don't get overly emotionally invested in something that you don't have a real plan to validate or be serious about later on."

Unfortunately, some college students – due to lack of knowledge or deceit – may say what they think the other person wants to hear. For example, a guy might say he wants a serious relationship, or a girl might say she is not necessarily looking for a serious relationship, but deep down they might honestly want the opposite.

Demerritt discourages that course of action. She warns, "You may find yourself in a pickle if you are not clear about your intentions." After finding out your partner's true intentions, you have a decision to make. She advises students to remain faithful to their desires.

She says, "You might find yourself making adjustments for that person. Eventually, you will find yourself resenting the person later." If a love interest says, "I just want to be friends, act accordingly," she advises. "You owe it to yourself to communicate the boundaries of friendship and stay within your limits. Don't think that because you allowed yourself to go beyond that limit that the friendship automatically evolves to a relationship." Remember, you have to take responsibility and protect yourself.

***

Building Blocks for Healthy Relationships

Some college relationships do lead to marriage. A Facebook study revealed that 29 percent of married couples met in college (though it does not say whether they were couples in college). Heavenly Kimes, DDS met her husband, Damon Kimes, M.D., while both were attending Meharry Medical College.

"I went there with the intention of getting my Doctor of Dental Surgery degree, DDS, and my MRS (colloquial for finding a husband)," shares Dr. Kimes, a star of Bravo TV's *Married to the Medicine* and author of *The Business of Love*. "I made a career and life plan. Part of that included my desire to meet my husband there and get married to a physician or a dentist."

The professional demands of dental and medical careers are emotionally and intellectually challenging. Dr. Kimes says it was helpful to have a mate that was professionally ambitious and understood her circumstances. Their relationship flourished because both were driven to accomplish their shared goals.

"I have been very fortunate that my husband and I mesh very well. He is a physician, I am a dentist, and we work together and support each other," she notes. "He paid for my first practice. We both contributed to his current practice. Our marriage is a partnership, and we treat it as such."

The former biology/pre-medicine student says her desire to have a family influenced her decision to become a dentist.

"First and foremost, I wanted to be a wife and a mother. In my mind, I thought if I became a physician, I would be on call and have to do a long residency. I always wanted to work part-time and have a great career, but still be a wife and mother," she shares. "I feel like I picked a career where I could do both. I could set my own hours. I did not have to do a long residency, and I could make great money as well."

Dr. Kimes says at her peak, her multidisciplinary dental practice annually generated $1.4 million. She has cut her clinical hours to raise her three children and support her physician husband of more than 20 years. Together, the Kimes family owns the Smiles by Dr. Heavenly dental practice, a pain management medical practice, and a host of insurance, real estate, and entrepreneurial interests.

Great relationships do not just happen by themselves. You must develop the skills and habits necessary to support and build a healthy and sustainable relationship. Chicago Metropolitan Battered Women's Network identifies many qualities of a healthy relationship (See: Table 14).

QUALITIES OF A HEALTHY RELATIONSHIP	
Fairness and Equality	• Being willing to compromise • Seeking goals that satisfy both partners
Fighting Fair	• Listening to each other • Avoiding assumptions • Not criticizing each other
Forgiveness	• Forgiving past mistakes • Admitting mistakes and apologizing
Good Communication	• Being honest about your feelings to yourself and your partner • Communicating openly and truthfully
Mutual Respect	• Listening without judgment • Valuing each other's opinions
Separate Identities	• Having friends outside the relationship • Exploring your individual identities
Trust and Support	• Respecting each other's personal space and time • Overcoming issues of jealousy and resentment

Table 14. SOURCE: Centralized Training Institute, Chicago Metropolitan Battered Women's Network "Teen Relationship Equality Wheel" and "Teen Power and Control Wheel"

***

Nine Tips for Productive Romantic Relationships

1. **LOVE AND RESPECT YOURSELF:** Being in a relationship will not save you from low self-esteem or loneliness. In many incidences, having a relationship can make your low self-esteem or loneliness worse. It is critical that you develop a healthy and empowering self-image. Always respect yourself. Never do or tolerate your partner doing anything that lowers your sense of self-worth or self-esteem. Attorney Francine Ward's *Esteemable Acts: 10 Actions for Building Real Self-Esteem* (Crown) is a great resource to help you strengthen your esteem.

2. **YOU ARE ONLY RESPONSIBLE FOR YOURSELF:** Do not allow your boyfriend or girlfriend to make you responsible for their education or wellbeing. It is not your responsibility to make sure they study, do their homework, or have groceries. It is not on you to make sure they eat, pay their bills, graduate, or get a job. Don't try to "save" someone who is not serious about his/her education or life. There is nothing wrong with giving your sweetie guidance or help, at times. Just make sure it is not holding you back in anyway. You need all of your energy to take care of your own life and educational obligations. Too many times, students feel stressed or pressured to feed their love interests or give them a ride somewhere. Avoid this at all costs. You may need to end the relationship if your sweetie does not understand. *The Success Principles: How to Get from Where You Are to Where You Want to Be* (William Morrow) by Jack Canfield and Janet Switzer offers practical guidance on taking responsibility for yourself.

3. **YOU CANNOT SAVE ANYONE BUT YOURSELF:** Sometimes, students may find their love partners in a long-term psychological funk or the person may have a toxic attitude. Demerritt says it is possible to support your partner without being emotionally down as well. Students must understand that they are not mental health professionals and do not have the capacity to "save" their partners. You must realize your limitations as a human being.

   Demerritt advises that you recommend your partner see a mental health professional. If your partner declines to seek professional help and the behavior continues, she says you may have to "disconnect from the relationship." Attempting to manage an emotionally and psychologically draining situation can negatively impact your quality of life and academic performance. *Get It Done When You're Depressed: 50 Strategies for Keeping Your Life on Track* (ALPHA) by Julie A. Fast and John D. Preston, Psy.D., is a helpful guide that advises readers about how to be productive despite experiencing depression.

4. **DO NOT BECOME FINANCIALLY INVOLVED:** Student loans are forever. It bears repeating – Student loans are FOREVER! In fact, student loans and credit scores often last longer than most college relationships. They are not going anywhere. You cannot discharge them in bankruptcy. You will pay them back, with interest. There is no escape! Lenders will garnish your paycheck or even take your income tax return, if necessary.

   Do not use student loans or credit cards to wine and dine or buy gifts for your partner. Do not accept, give, or exchange expensive (more than $25) gifts. In fact, $25 should be the most money you spend on anything involving your partner. Be careful with loaning your car, money, and other expensive items.

Be careful about sharing your family's financial information or lifestyle. Some people prey on students they perceive are from affluent households. They scope the type of cars, jewelry, clothes, and accessories people have and plot to get access to these items. *Financial Lovemaking: Merging Assets with Your Partner in Ways That Feel Good* (Blue Boy Publishing Company) by Dr. Boyce Watkins can help you create a healthy balance in this area.

5. **BE PREPARED AND PROTECT YOURSELF**: College campuses all over the world are filled with minimally supervised students, raging hormones, sexual energy, and curiosity. If you decide to become sexually active, be prepared and protect yourself. Many former college students contend with the consequences of Sexually Transmitted Diseases (STD), abortions, miscarriages, false paternity claims, and deadbeat co-parents. These things can become a hurdle to graduating on time and have a long-term impact on your life.

    Stanford University's Sexual Health Peer Resource Center reveals that 1-in-4 college students have an STD. If you do decide to become sexually active, act as though everyone – including your sweetie – has a sexually transmitted disease. It is your body, your life, and your future. You cannot take a person's word for it. Take STD screenings regularly. Have and use contraceptives. Your sexuality and health are precious. Once you give them away, you cannot take them back.

    Be discreet. Keep people out of your business. Your friends are not entitled to know the intimate details of your romantic and sexual escapades. Edmond and Green's *Loving in the Grown Zone: A No-Nonsense Guide to Making Healthy Decisions in the Quest for Loving, Romantic Relationships of Honor, Esteem, and Respect*

(Balboa Press) offers insight that can help you define grown love for yourself.

6. **FORGIVE YOURSELF**: Edmond and Green say being grown and loving yourself means you are able to forgive yourself for past slipups and poor decisions. They encourage their followers to make, "the next decision better." Edmond concedes that many people have a little "adult mess," or past relationship regrets and mishaps. Green says, "You always have the ability to make a better decision," regardless of your mistakes or how poorly you may have treated a past lover. Demerritt's *Push Past Pain to Purpose: A Self-Help Guide to Overcoming Past Hurts and Embracing Your Life's Purpose* will give you tools to help you move beyond regrets.

7. **TAKE YOUR TIME**: Avoid U-Hauling (the phenomenon of a relationship moving way too quickly to the point where you have practically moved in together after only a few weeks). Don't trust easily. Let your love interest earn your trust, but don't be paranoid either. Observe what your partner says. Allow them to verify what they say with action over time. Evaluate their character. Remember Edmond's and Green's advice to limit access to your body, money, house, and heart while you are assessing prospects. Sometimes in relationships, we may wonder, "How did I end up with this person?" or "What did I see in him/her?" Limiting access can help you see them more objectively. Limit phone time with the person. You may not want them to be the first or last person you talk to each day because doing so can have the person at the forefront of your mind or have a subconscious impact. In the case of breakups, give yourself time to heal and regain emotional strength before engaging in new relationships. *How to be Your Own Best Friend (Random House)* by Mildred Newman, M.A. and Bernard Berkowitz, Ph.D., offers insights into embracing and using your personal power.

8. **DO NOT LEAD PEOPLE ON:** It is unfair to allow a person to love you if you do not feel the same way about them. It is equally unfair to allow a person to woo you with time, gifts or acts to impress you when you have no romantic interest in them. Be clear and direct with the person and communicate that you are not romantically interested in them. Although the person may be disappointed, if they are mature they will respect the fact that you did not lead them on or allow them to make a fool of themselves.

9. **BE PATIENT, LOVE WILL REVEAL ITSELF:** Many students may be ashamed to be single. The Independent Women's Forum (IWF) shows that 30 percent (nearly 6 million) of college students have been on fewer than two dates. While doing research for their book *Premarital Sex in America: How Young Americans Meet, Mate, and Think About Marrying* (Oxford University Press), authors Mark Regnerus and Jeremy Uecker discovered that 12 percent of females (more than 2 million) and 13 percent of males (roughly 2.25 million) were virgins. Edmond and Green encourage you to avoid pressure to get into a relationship or to have sex. Edmond notes, "So many people feel pressured to be in a relationship or have sex just because they don't want people to think they are corny." Green says your ability to stand alone and appreciate your individuality gives you the power to love yourself and become successful in college and life.

VSU President Dr. Abdullah assures that there are rewards for being yourself. "Honestly, if you commit to being who you are you will attract friends and significant others that like and appreciate the real you," Dr. Abdullah offers. "Don't let anything stop you from graduating."

Approach love with patience and caution. Remember, college is your chance to position yourself to compete for advanced educational and career opportunities. Finding that special someone is a bonus.

***

Lethal Cocktail: Love and Violence

> "She was in love and I'd ask her how? I mean why?
> What kind of love from a person would black your
> eye? What kind of love from a person every night
> make you cry? What kind of love from a person
> make you wish he would die?"
>
> — **Rapper Eve**, "Love is Blind"
> (Ruff Ryders Entertainment, Interscope Records)

The National Coalition Against Domestic Violence (NCADV) notes that 21 percent of college students (2.2 million) report dating violence by a current love interest. We are all too familiar with the various justifications and explanations:

- I love my sweetie, and we have a cool relationship, but sometimes she gets furious at me and curses me out."
- "My baby is overall a wonderful person, but has a bad temper."
- "When things are chaotic, he'll pop off and call me 'bitch,' 'slut,' or 'whore.'"
- "Only a few times he grabbed me roughly. Nothing major."
- "He has to have the last word, and sometimes he slaps me to make sure I am listening."
- "The situation is complicated, that's why I keep my business to myself. I don't share too much with my friends. They always jump to conclusions."
- "Everybody has problems. Nobody's perfect."

The story of Brandie James (*not her real name*) captures much of the drama that unravels a student-victim's life. Brandie came to college already in a two-year relationship with her hometown boyfriend Howard, (*not his real name*) who was three years older. Brandie was a student in a highly competitive five-year advanced graduate degree program. When they arrived in town, Howard started working at a fast food restaurant and living off campus in his own apartment.

As Brandie excelled in school, she began to notice little changes in Howard. She remembers him always downplaying her personal victories. Howard often manipulated Brandie psychologically, masking his aggression as protection. Things progressively went downhill, but Brandie's emotional attachment to him influenced her to maintain their toxic connection. A turning point happened during her junior year. Although Brandie survived her painful experience with domestic violence, recalling the encounter still brings tears to her eyes more than a dozen years later:

> "He was my first real boyfriend and my first sexual experience. I was not ready to let him go. My parents tried to tell me not to take him with me to college, but I didn't listen. He made me feel so good like I was this mature woman when in reality I was just young, dumb, and in love.
>
> I was doing great in school, meeting new people, and started to develop confidence and spread my wings socially. It seemed like the better I performed in school, the more jealous he got. He began saying I was going to leave him and go with one of those college boys.
>
> He would say things like, 'I don't want you to hang with so-and-so because she is bad news,' or 'you can't go to this event because you never know what can pop off.' Here I was, thinking he was protective when in actuality he was controlling me.
>
> One day, I remember disagreeing with him about something simple. He yelled at me and squeezed me really hard. I remember him screaming, 'Don't think you are better than me!' He saw me crying. Then, he started crying. He said, 'I am sorry. I love you. Why do you think

I am working hard at this fast food restaurant? I am doing it for you.'

The abuse eventually got worse. Howard started hitting me more often. I didn't know any better and I was afraid to challenge him. I was still in love with him and I felt that it was my fault. He had me thinking that I was stressing him and putting him down.

[One day] We were arguing, and I just said, "I am tired of arguing, I'm sick of you hitting me, and I can't take this anymore!" Then, he said, 'Oh yeah? After all, I've done for you?' He threw me into a wall in my room. He threw me hard enough that my body went through drywall. My head hit the wooden 4x4 part and my back and arm hit the cement bags that they put between sheetrock.

That was the end of everything with him. I felt so embarrassed, scared, and ashamed at the same time. I sprained my back and had to get a cast on my arm. I never told my parents about the previous incidences. My roommate would always ask if I needed help, and I would always tell her I was ok and to mind her business.

It is not okay if your partner belittles you or becomes aggressive with you. If you find yourself lying to your parents and friends that may be a warning sign that you need to get out of that relationship."

Abuse is an unfortunate reality for some college students, yet it is a fact too many choose to ignore. Whether physical or emotional, abuse is as terrifying as it is unimaginable. NCADV research points out:

- More than half of domestic violence victims were abused by a current or former boyfriend or girlfriend.
- 21 percent of college students report having experienced dating violence by a current partner.

- 32 percent experienced dating violence by a previous partner.
- More than 13 percent of college women report they have been stalked. Of those, 42 percent were stalked by a boyfriend or ex-boyfriend.

Abuse is dreadfully complicated and should never be tolerated. Your only healthy choice is to place your own safety first. If you are in a violent relationship, there are things you can do that may increase your security and assist you in ending the relationship.

Break the Cycle, Inc. (www.BreakingTheCycle.org), a youth dating abuse awareness organization, and "Prevention of Dating Violence on College Campuses: An Innovative Program," an article in the *Journal of College Counseling* (American College Counseling Association), highlight several warning signs of domestic abuse (See: Table 15).

Domestic violence is nothing to be ashamed of. Abuse has no gender. If you are in an abusive relationship, you have many options including calling your campus police department and getting a restraining order against your attacker. On-campus students can ask the housing office for relocation. You can also call the confidential 24/7 National Domestic Violence Hotline at 1-800-799-7233. Inform your friends, find support from others, and put a safety plan into action.

***

Rape and the College Student

66 *"No means no! It's not your job to get her to say yes. If the woman says no, and you don't listen to her, it's rape. Plain and simple. Case closed."*
— **Comedian Sinbad**, portraying Walter Oaks,
"A Different World television series"
(Casey-Werner Productions) 99

The Federal Bureau of Investigation's (FBI) Uniform Crime Report (UCR) Summary Reporting System (SRS) defines forcible sexual assault as, *"The penetration, no matter how slight, of the vagina or anus with any body part or object, or oral penetration by a sex organ of another person without the consent of the victim."* Some jurisdictions include unwanted or forcible touching in their rape statutes. In several jurisdictions, attempted rape or even threatened rape is a statutory crime.

DOMESTIC ABUSE WARNING SIGNS

Checking cell phones, emails or social networks	Making threats to hurt themselves, you, or your friends and family	Unwilling to accept responsibility for abuse
Extreme jealousy or insecurity	Unpredictable mood swings	Forced sex or affection
Constant belittling or put-downs	Physically inflicting pain or hurt in any way	Playing mental games
Explosive temper	Possessiveness	Displaying weapons
Isolation from family and friends	Telling someone what to do	Taking and keeping your property
Making false accusations	Drugging or getting you drunk	Destroying your property
Making you believe they are the only one who cares about you	Limiting your activities outside the relationship	Making you afraid to wear certain clothes or makeup

Table 15. SOURCE: Break the Cycle, Inc., and "Prevention of Dating Violence on College Campuses: An Innovative Program," *Journal of College Counseling.*

According to judicial data, sex crime penalties from both the federal and state systems include six to seven years of prison time. Rape convictions carry more severe penalties, averaging eight to 10 years of prison time. Some convictions include probation and registering as a sexual predator or offender.

The National Institute of Justice's "Sexual Victimization of College Women" report uncovered that:

- Approximately 20 to 25 percent of college women experience a completed or attempted rape over the course of their college career.

- Less than 5 percent of rape or attempted rape victims report the occurrence to law enforcement.

- The majority (two-thirds) of victims told another person, usually a friend, not a family member or school official.

- Off-campus sexual victimization is more common among college women than on-campus victimization. Of victims of completed rape, 33.7 percent were victimized on campus, and 66.3 percent occurred off campus.

NCADV data adds:

- Among college students who were sexually assaulted, 35 percent of **attempted** rapes took place during dates, 22 percent of **threatened** rapes happened during dates, and 12 percent of **completed** rapes occurred on dates.

- 13 percent of college women report they were forced to have sex by a dating partner.

To be clear, no one is entitled to non-consensual sex with anyone under any circumstance. This may provoke a few questions:

Q: What if two lovers had consensual sex before and one decides that they don't want to have sex this time?
A: It is rape if one partner forces the experience on the other without their permission, regardless of prior consent.

Q: What if two lovers are consensually engaging in one type of sex and one partner wants to initiate another kind of sex?
A: It is rape if the other lover did not give the interested party permission to proceed.

Q: What if we are both intoxicated and one lover wants to have sex?
A: It is rape if the partner did not give the interested party permission to proceed.

In some cases, consent is explicit. In other *"perceived"* areas, the lines of permission might seem gray. If you are unsure about your partner's consent, please do not proceed. It is better to go home free and disappointed than to break the law and forfeit your future and freedom.

Silence may well be golden, but not when sexual assault or rape is involved. Rape is very often a private crisis for college students who find themselves exposed to sexual violence from within their social circles. Socialized to believe that you do not "air your dirty laundry," many students silently endure the shameful trauma in isolation. The frequency of rape is not entirely known because too many victims do not tell people who can help them.

The repercussions of the devastating event might not hit right away, but sexual violence has a particularly significant impact on its victims. Various mental health experts and data note severe long-term psychological symptoms can linger for years. Some victims experience anger and rage, chronic anxiety, depression, isolation, exhaustion, flashbacks and recurring nightmares, social withdrawal, an inability to concentrate, irritability, paranoia, and a hostile, cynical, and distrustful attitude toward the world many years after the attack. Everyone responds differently to trauma and struggle to find ways to cope and function (See: Mind, Body, and Soul).

Rape is an illogical act that can cause a person not to function normally. There are many resources (both campus and non-campus affiliated) you can use to navigate this painful experience. They include your campus police station, the college health center, the local hospital, the National Sexual Assault Hotline at 1-800-656-HOPE (4673), and National Sexual Violence Resource Center at 1-877-739-3895.

Sexual assault – attempted, threatened, or completed – is a crime. No one deserves to be raped. No clothing item, social setting, or an individual's perceived reputation invites anyone to rape someone. No one invites or deserves to be raped.

IACM SAFETY SUGGESTIONS

SITUATIONS	POSSIBLE APPROACHES
Walking Alone at Night	Walk in groups or call campus resources such as Safe Team escorts and trusted friends to accompany you to your car or destination.
Dating	Try using group dates or public events to socialize with your love interests. Vet your love interests before going on one-on-one dates. Let at least three people know with whom you are going out and the location.
Intoxication	Advertisers encourage drinkers to do so responsibility. IACM does not endorse any substances. Intoxication can alter your thinking, behavior, and reaction abilities.
Group Settings	Avoid being alone in private group settings that include people who are unknown to you. These types of unfamiliar environments may have the potential to breed group assault.
Rape or Attempted Rape	Immediately call law enforcement. Do not shower. File a police report or legal complaint. Engage a mental health professional. You may eventually decide to consult an attorney.

Table 16.

***

Exit Strategies: Breaking Up is Hard to Do

❝ *"Think it's best we go our separate ways.*
Tell me why I should stay in this relationship,
When I'm hurting baby. I ain't happy baby,
Plus, there's so many other things I gotta deal with.
I think that you should let it burn."
— **Usher**, "Let it Burn"
(Sony Music Entertainment) ❞

Dr. Abdullah has spent more than 20 years of his professional life on college campuses. In his experience, many students encounter their first strong relationship during their first semester on campus.

"Now students can spend more time with their love interest than they could at home. They can spend 24 hours with the person if they want to," Dr. Abdullah observes. "The idea that the relationship might not work out – and it's almost guaranteed not to work out – can be devastating."

He says a student's ability to emotionally and academically work through a relationship's demise can go a long way toward a successful life. "How students react and bounce back from a breakup will dictate how they approach their college career," he offers. "If you can study through a breakup and get good grades through a breakup, you will do well in college."

The VSU president notes getting over a love interest may cause some students to close themselves off from their family, friends, and educational responsibilities.

Dr. Abdullah implores, "Don't stop studying and don't stop doing the things you need to do to graduate."

Knowing how and when to dissolve a relationship is the most critical skill for anyone seeking a relationship. You have to be mature, conscious, and courageous enough to disconnect from an unhealthy relationship or even a healthy relationship that is distracting you from your education, which is your primary goal.

When you decide to leave, leave for real. Know that your feelings will not instantly disappear. The memories – both good and bad – will not immediately fade away. Make sure you allow yourself time to heal from the breakup. You may want to limit communication or access to your previous partner until you have stabilized your emotions. Resist every urge to act or publicly lash out.

Demerritt adds, "You have to evaluate your emotions to find out if you truly want to break up with your partner. Only you can determine whether the relationship is healthy or productive for you. If you decide to move forward, you may want to engage a therapist or counselor to help you work through the issue emotionally."

Demerritt warns it is important to thoughtfully and carefully work through your emotions when considering a breakup. She says doing so helps you avoid making an emotional decision you may regret later. Demerritt offers guidance on popular breakup causes:

- DOMESTIC VIOLENCE: "In cases of domestic violence, you want to develop an exit plan so you can safely exit the relationship. That may mean engaging law enforcement to file a report to make them aware of your fears and desire to leave an abusive relationship. It may mean going to court and filing a restraining order. You have to be willing to engage all necessary resources so that you can exit the situation safely."

- RAPE: "Rape or attempted rape is a reason to terminate a relationship."

- INFIDELITY: "If there are cheating concerns, you have to go through a mental process within yourself where you arrive at the conclusion that this is not healthy for me. Infidelity is often a difficult one. People often blame themselves instead of the individual who cheated. Some people get overly emotional or get aggressive towards their partner. When the infidelity is sexual, you might be exposed to diseases, so you have to determine if staying involved is the healthiest choice for you."

- **MISMATCHED VALUES**: "This happens a lot when you bring high school relationships to college. People engage in different beliefs, habits, and ways of life. You have to decide what is best for your future. You may come to the conclusion that what's important to your partner is not important for you. Sometimes, this leads to breakups."

- **SELFISH PARTNERS**: "In college, you have to do what is best for you, especially if the relationship is not serious, but if you and your partner agreed to a committed relationship, you have to be able to do what is best for the relationship. If your partner is more concerned about themselves, then you have a choice on whether you can continue your involvement with this person in that manner."

Demerritt advises honest communication in practically all breakup cases. She warns, "So many people lie about the reason they want to end a relationship. This is not good."

She points out that being honest with your partner is about self-respect. Lastly, she adds there are very few painless breakups.

"Unfortunately, there is pain involved, but you have to do what is in your best interest and what's best for your partner," she adds.

You do not have to remain in an unsafe or unproductive relationship. If you have difficulty building up the nerve to break up with your partner, connect with a mental health counselor (See: Mind, Body, and Soul).

CHAPTER 10

ARE YOU READY FOR A
21ˢᵀ CENTURY CAREER?

> 66 *"Do not primarily train men to work. Train them to serve willingly and intelligently."*
> — **James "J.C." Cash Penney**, American Entrepreneur, Founder, J.C. Penney stores 99

The global job market is competitive. Companies fill vacancies with applicants who possess a desired level of skills and experiences. In a series of detailed surveys, the National Association of Colleges and Employers (NACE), an association that connects college career services professionals with the business community, examined the skill requirements of 144 leading companies. The participating businesses identified criteria used to evaluate prospective job candidates. The results identified seven "must have" skills needed to get hired (See: Table 17):

1. Critical Thinking and Problem Solving
2. Professionalism and Work Ethic
3. Teamwork
4. Oral and Written Communication
5. Information Technology Application
6. Leadership
7. Career Management

You can learn the basics. But, developing the attitudes, perspectives, and self-assessments conducive to the professional world can be challenging. Despite the challenges, maximizing your potential is worth the effort.

The transition from student to emerging professional can bring many complexities that take time and effort to master. NACE experts recommend students begin building career skills through school clubs and organizations, work-study programs, volunteering and day-to-day errands on campus.

SEVEN MUST HAVE SKILLS TO GET HIRED

DESIRED SKILLS	IACM TRANSLATION
Critical Thinking & Problem Solving	Can you size up a situation and come up with a solution without much supervision? Do you know the right time to activate your boss? Do you come to the boss with problems or solutions? Can you mature to a place where you can anticipate issues and create solutions ahead of time?
Professionalism & Work Ethic	Do you perform your job in a pleasant and considerate way? Are you willing to do what it takes to complete the task?
Teamwork	Can you work with others? Do you add value to the team?
Oral & Written Communication	Are you able to organize your thoughts in a clear and concise way? Do you convey all of the necessary information at the appropriate time?
Technology Application	Can you competently use systems to produce quality work?
Leadership	Are you competent? Can you influence other people (inside and outside of the team or company) to produce the desired solution?
Career Management	Are you acquiring the needed tools, skills, relationships and experiences to help the company grow?

Table 17. SOURCE: NACE Career Readiness Survey

Through these activities, students can develop the ability to interact with others in appropriate ways, learn simple skills related to work ethic, and begin to develop relationships with influential people on campus. Use your time on campus to build an excellent reputation that inspires confidence and credibility.

Students should be engaged at their college in a way that leaves a lasting legacy. How you helped improve or enhance your institution will be part of the story you share when interviewing with employers. This demonstrates to employers that you are the kind of person who makes a difference. That is a compelling story to share.

***

Critical Thinking and Problem-Solving

Students develop critical thinking and problem-solving skills through their academic experiences because many of the courses require those skills to successfully complete assignments, case studies, and curriculum requirements.

Although it is impossible for a person to know everything or for a person to create solutions without having accurate information, exercising critical thinking will prevent you from telling your boss or colleagues, "I don't know" – three words that can undermine your professional credibility.

The workplace is a dynamic environment. Two of the greatest benefits of the college experience are learning how to seek credible information, and understanding how to create desired solutions. It is your job to observe those dynamics and use your critical thinking and problem-solving skills to consistently deliver results.

You may ask, well if it is impossible to know everything, what is wrong with saying, I don't know? Understand, you were hired and paid to find out. You are there to adequately size up situations and determine a course of action that produces desired results. That process is called critical thinking. Instead of saying I don't know, consider saying, "I'd like to revisit that after I organize my thoughts," or, "There are a few ways we can approach this situation. I will weigh out the pros and cons and come back to you with the best plan." If something is not within your area of understanding, you could say, "Molly might be the best person to help us come up with a solution for this. That is her area of expertise."

While the classroom environment is entirely different from the workplace, students can use internships and work-study opportunities to familiarize themselves with the dynamics of the professional environment. Remember, internships are still first and foremost learning experiences. Being comfortable in these environments stimulates better performance.

Ultimately, regardless of your position, you were hired to solve problems and create solutions. In *Critical Thinking Tactics for Nurses,* authors M. Gaie Rubenfeld, R.N., M.S., and Barbara K. Scheffer, R.N., Ed.D., outline the critical thinking process into seven skills: Analyzing, Applying, Discriminating, Information Seeking, Logical Reasoning, Predicting, and Transforming Knowledge (See: Table 18).

Students can increase their critical thinking skills by enrolling in an on-campus critical thinking course or philosophy class, or by practicing Scheffer and Rubenfeld's "Seven Critical Thinking Skills," that can be found on the University of Michigan's Thoughts on Problem Solving site (See: Appendix C).

***

Professionalism

> " *"Professionalism is not sportsmanship. If you don't succeed, you won't be in your profession for long."*
> — **Charles Theodore "Chili" Davis,**
> Former Major League Baseball Player "

If you ask a dozen people to define professionalism, you might get twelve different answers. Still, it is necessary to understand that essential professional characteristics include proper appearance (clothing, grooming, and body language), upbeat attitude, responsiveness, and competence. The late John H. Johnson, owner, and CEO of Johnson Publishing Company (JPC), called it "going first class."

SCHEFFER AND RUBENFELD'S SEVEN CRITICAL THINKING SKILLS

Analyzing	Can you break down a whole situation into parts and understand how they work and connect to each other?
Applying Standards	Do you know how to come up with solutions that match or exceed the best practices in your industry?
Discriminating	Are you learning to make out the differences and similarities among things or situations? Can you put them in categories?
Information Seeking	Can you search for relevant and credible information to help you come up with viable solutions?
Logical Reasoning	Are your thoughts and conclusions supported by credible proof?
Predicting	Can you assess a situation and create a plan? Do you understand the consequences?
Transforming Knowledge	Are you able to use what you know, learned and researched? Can you use that information to create better solutions?

Table 18. SOURCE: B. K. Scheffer and M.G. Rubenfeld, "A Consensus Statement on Critical Thinking in Nursing," *Journal of Nursing Education, 39,* 352-9 *(2000)*; B. K. Scheffer and M.G. Rubenfeld, "Critical Thinking: What Is It and How Do We Teach It?," *Current Issues in Nursing,* J.M. Grace, Rubl, H.K. (2001).

"For as long as I can remember, I've been fascinated by the idea of going first class. It's a part of my operating philosophy," Johnson wrote in his best-selling memoir, *Succeeding Against the Odds: The Autobiography of a Great American Businessman*

(JPC). "It informs my view of men, women, events, and the world."

Johnson described going first class as performing with, "class, style, grace, elegance, and excellence." Your goal is to earn the confidence of your peers and clientele with your ability to execute your tasks well and do them in first-class fashion. That means spending time with others and building stable relationships. It also means seizing any opportunity to go beyond the call of duty. You also help others to work in a more meaningful, fulfilling, and happy way. You also perform your job in a pleasurable manner free of pain.

Pain free means working with seriousness, and turning in error-free work on time – preferably early. Your final product reflects quality and great consideration. It also means taking the time to consider your employer, co-workers, and clients. With customers, you demonstrate a courteous and pleasant demeanor while communicating with them, setting expectations, and promptly providing desired solutions. With colleagues, you respect their expertise and do all that you reasonably can to help them win in the workplace, within your scope of work.

In short, first-class professionalism is using all of your skills and personality to complete assignments with excellence and grace. Professional standards differ depending on the workplace and industry. Professionalism and execution are critical to you accomplishing your professional goals.

A few elements of professional performance you can use when starting a new job or internship include: Learn, Apply, Master, and Anticipate (See: Table 20).

Having lofty professional ambitions is commendable. You have big goals and want all of the good things in life. The only way to reach those benchmarks is by hard work and commitment to excellence. Yale trained physician, Dr. Benjamin Carson encourages students to, "Develop the talents God has given you so that you can become more valuable to your fellow man."

IACM PROFESSIONAL VALUES FOR CAREER SUCCESS

ALWAYS	
Stay in professional "character." Always maintain the professional decorum that reflects your personal and the organization's code of conduct and ethics.	Treat clients with meticulous care. Be polite, pleasant, and smile. Infuse each encounter with your unique emotions and sensitivities. Take notice and honor each person's humanity by promptly acknowledging his/her presence and advising the person that someone will be with them shortly.
Always maintain professional distance with co-workers and clients. You are there to perform a job, not to socialize. It is more important to garner respect for superior work performance versus being known for your personality or anything else.	Respect your boss's authority and direction. Move forward with a positive attitude, even if you disagree with their directed course of action. Part of being a professional is being able to create the desired professional solutions, regardless of your personal feelings.
Always have the necessary items for work, (e.g., badge, keys, pens, paper, materials, etc.) It may seem minor, but continued offenses will diminish peer confidence in you.	Take ownership of your work, personal brand, and organization. Emerging professionals avoid the "that's not my job" vibe by taking pride in themselves and their service.
Always have a positive attitude. If you borrow an item from an employee, always return it in a timely fashion and in the exact place you received it.	Maintain integrity, honesty, and high standards for yourself. Always communicate truthfully and honestly. Take responsibility for mishaps. Avoid excessive personal phone calls.

Table 19.

It's not what you do, but how you do it. So, with enthusiasm, care and precision, push yourself to reach your highest possibilities. Others will notice, and you will gain more respect from your colleagues. You can leverage that respect for greater responsibilities and opportunities. Success is the reward for working hard. Hard work is a noble aspiration. You will appreciate your career and develop a greater sense of self-esteem. Besides, it feels much better when your goals are honestly earned.

Fair warning, laziness and a poor work ethic can unravel all of your professional efforts and reputation. Most career experts agree that it is hard to take a lazy colleague seriously. It is equally hard to justify giving a lazy person a raise or promotion.

IACM ELEMENTS OF PROFESSIONAL WORK EXECUTION	
DO	**TRANSLATION**
Learn	Use your honeymoon period as an intern or new hire to learn about the company's culture, history, and way of doing things (e.g., communicating with the boss, turning in assignments on time, and learning the way co-workers collaborate on tasks).
Apply	Practice and demonstrate what you learned. This helps prove that you are a good hire, that you belong in the environment, and add value to the team.
Master	Now that you have a grasp on the environment, you must show that you can consistently perform at a high level. Consistency is the optimal word.
Anticipate	After you have mastered your job, you can begin to plan possible solutions when there are mishaps. And, you can predict how long it takes you to complete assignments. Understanding the time needed to complete tasks gives you a tremendous advantage because now you can effectively communicate processes and set and manage expectations on the job.

Table 20.

REMEMBER THESE FIVE GOLDEN NUGGETS:

1. When you have two choices, be very weary of choosing the easier option. Many times laziness inspires choosing the easier option.

2. The lazy option will at first appear to offer comfort and ease. In the long run, however, a lazy professional will become irrelevant and dispensable. Their work life will become meaningless and mediocre.

3. Laziness is a huge barrier when it comes to self-acceptance and finding the energy to pursue or work on goals and ambitions.

4. German-born diarist Anne Frank wrote, "Laziness may appear attractive, but work gives satisfaction."

5. French writer Pierre-Jules Renard opined, "Failure is not our only punishment for laziness. There is also the success of others."

***

Work Ethic

   "No excuse is acceptable. No amount of effort is adequate until proven effective."
     — **Sybil C. Mobley, Ph.D.,** Founding Dean,
Florida A&M University School of
Business and Industry

Hip-hop mogul Russell Simmons grew up in a middle-class, two-parent family in Queens, New York. Simmons co-founded several iconic companies including Def Jam Records (1983), Phat Farm Clothing (1992), and the Rush Card (2003), among others. The multi-millionaire entrepreneur and philanthropist says there are no shortcuts to success, not even for himself.

"Work very hard and be so aggressive that you show up every day," says Simmons, author of *Do You!: 12 Laws to Access the Power in You to Achieve Happiness and Success* (Avery). "You inspire your bosses when you come to work earlier than them and leave after them."

Simmons has a reported net worth of more than $300 million and jokes that you must hustle like an immigrant. "People come to this country from shanty houses in Cape Town, South Africa. They know that is a real struggle and this (America) is a place of opportunity," he says. "So, they put their heads down and get to work."

The son of two Howard University graduates discloses that if you work hard and embrace your moment your work will become your reward. "The fruit of your labor is that you are happy while you are working on it. There is nothing like being focused and committed while you are working. The excitement makes you happy, and that's your payment," he reveals. "Money doesn't make you happy, but happy makes money."

Simmons concludes, "It's better to work than to sit at home. Sitting at home is boring, but to really be successful you have to be involved in your work every day."

Work ethics including following through with job responsibilities, showing up on time, and working hard are must-have qualities for career success. Executing quality work ethic is not painstakingly difficult. It is using your time, effort, and skills to produce first-class work without excuses. It is a personal commitment to doing whatever (ethically, morally, and legally) is necessary (e.g., staying later, coming in earlier, pitching in on an assignment, and helping team members) to complete tasks on time with excellence – not halfway done or almost done, but done with excellence. Bosses and clients will not care if you labored all night if you have not created the desired result.

CONSIDER THESE TWO TIPS FOR BOOSTING YOUR HAPPINESS AND WORK ETHIC:

- Master simple things at work and consciously appreciate every opportunity to evolve as a professional.

- Pinpoint some assignments at work, and set aside a few minutes – at the end the day – to contemplate and feel gratitude for your contributions as part of the team.

***

Teamwork

> " *"Coming together is a beginning; keeping together is progress; working together is success."*
> — **Henry Ford,** Founder, Ford Motor Company " "

The workplace consists of many sophisticated dynamics including interpersonal relationships and existing team operation methods. Effective employees first enter job environments observing and understanding the dynamics of how their team works and then work within that structure.

Employers evaluate several candidates before hiring. They assume the top candidates have the desired skills. The deciding factor is often figuring out which candidate is the best fit for the organization.

Use your first weeks on the job to find out the chain of command, how your division impacts the organization's bottom line, how your supervisor prefers you communicate with them, how your team operates, how employees turn in assignments, and how to access company training. Work within the set structure, not outside of it.

Demonstrate that you respect the structure and processes already in place. For example, if your supervisor prefers e-mail communication versus one-on-one meetings, send concise yet detailed e-mails. If the team collaborates on Basecamp and teleconferences, you must become proficient at those platforms and use them exclusively.

Although a supervisor may not offer the same structure a professor provided, emerging professionals must still be able to accomplish workplace goals within the existing dynamics of the job culture. This can prove challenging for inexperienced employees filled with many bright ideas and interesting ways to do things. That is why it is important that new hires resist the urge to try and change things immediately.

Supervisors and co-workers may consider you unprofessional, spoiled, or rude if you always criticize and challenge a proven process or structure that has reliably produced desired results. The only way to earn the right to make a humble suggestion is after accomplishing two things:

1. Earning the respect and confidence of your supervisor and co-workers.

2. Mastering the current way of conducting business.

Then, and only then, can you make one – not several – recommendations at a time.

Team morale and chemistry is another concern among employers. Use your time in campus clubs and organizations and during group assignments to strengthen your team building skills.

Displaying professional friendliness (being approachable and coachable when necessary), consideration for co-workers and clients, and having a pleasant attitude are needed for team chemistry.

Conflict among employees can decrease chemistry and morale. Priscilla Dames, M.S., chief executive officer of Wingspan Seminars, LLC, a conflict resolution firm, encourages employees to be builders and not dividers.

"Conflict resolution is community building," explains Dames, a graduate of Ball State University. "Your work environment is a community. Multiple teams are working in that community."

Supervisors typically do not want to settle disputes between employees. The Indiana native notes, "According to industry data, managers spend about 34 percent of their time trying to resolve conflicts." She says it has a negative impact on the bottom line.

The longtime conflict management expert says many conflicts often arise out misunderstandings and misperception. "Our job is to deescalate conflicts. If not, we will lose productivity, workforce morale, and money," Dames shares. "When we build positive alliances, everybody benefits. We must all understand that we are trying to improve the overall bottom line. A positive workforce boosts productivity and profits."

Dames' endorses these tips to resolve conflicts in the workplace.

- **FIND COMMON GROUND**: "It is very important to know and understand the organization's mission and goal. When everyone is on the same page, we can move forward together."

- **HONOR AND PLAY BY THE RULES**: "Anytime you want to resolve conflicts, you have to understand the rules of dealing with conflicts in your professional environment. Most organizations have Human Resources departments. Use the HR department to find out the appropriate ways to manage conflicts at your job."

- **RESPECT DIFFERENCES**: "There are so many differences in the workplace ranging from age, sex, culture, religion, and perspective. Be patient and open-minded. Embracing workplace diversity can expand your worldview and enhance your career."

- **COMMUNICATION IS KEY**: "Communication is huge. Establishing a relationship starts with communication. You have to consider your tone and language when talking to people. Communication facilitates understanding on both sides."

- **REMEMBER YOUR GOALS**: "You must always ask yourself, 'What's in it for me?' If you want longevity at your job, you have to learn to work with your colleagues. Relationships are a major part of your success. Relating to your colleagues on a professional level helps you focus on what they really want out of the work experience. This mentality helps you succeed in that environment."

***

Oral and Written Communication

❝ *"You can have brilliant ideas, but if you can't get them across, your ideas won't get you anywhere."*
— **Lee Iacocca,** Iconic Executive,
Former CEO, Chrysler ❞

Motivational speaker Les Brown was born into poverty in Miami's Liberty City community in 1945. Brown struggled financially for much of his early and young adult life. Brown says developing his communication skills helped him rise out of poverty and earn more than $60 million in the professional speaking industry.

"Cultivating your communications skills increases your quality of life in your career and your profession," says Brown, author of the best-selling *Live Your Dreams* (Harper Collins). "Your ability to communicate and relate to people is critical to your success."

The world-renowned orator stresses that communication is not just about speaking. "You have to engage your partner and build understanding. You also have to create understanding and develop insight into the people you are communicating with on an everyday basis," he continues. "It is about listening and building relationships."

When someone says something of importance, try to "listen" by taking the time to think about your relationship with the person who is speaking. By actively listening with the relationship in mind you will know just how to react and be able to give the person precisely what they need.

Brown says successful communication strengthens relationships, builds teamwork, and boosts confidence. He adds, "You want to be able to relate to people in a way that inspires cooperation. This allows you to build trust and collaborate for individual and collective goals."

Emerging professionals can use campus-oriented resources to learn suitable communication techniques for their future workplaces. Students can also engage alumni who work in their desired profession as mentors to help coach them on how to express themselves professionally.

Lindsay Olson, a New York-based publicist, developed 10 top communication tips.

You can develop your speaking skills by enrolling in courses for public speaking, theater, or dialogue. You can also join a local chapter of Toastmasters International.

Oral and written communication are valuable skills needed to succeed in the modern workplace. Mastering these abilities will help you realize your professional dreams.

LINDSAY OLSON'S 10 TOP COMMUNICATION TIPS

1. **Listen:** Most of us are terrible listeners. Instead of truly listening to what the person is saying, we interrupt, prepare our response, or think we already know what the speaker is going to say next. It is impossible to understand what someone needs or wants if we do not give them our undivided attention.	2. **Pay Attention to Body Language:** Body language can tell you just as much as what a person says, if not more. Observe how they act when they talk. Is your co-worker saying she can meet a deadline, but wringing her hands while she says it? She might be afraid to tell you it will be hard to make the due date.
3. **Consider Communication Preference:** Not everyone likes to communicate the same way. Email works for some, but others would rather pick up the phone and talk, text, or even use social media or instant messaging to relay something. Respect the person you're trying to contact and use the method she seems to prefer. If you've called a client several times and always get her voicemail, but she's always quick to respond to email, switch to email instead.	4. **Consider Your Tone:** The problem with email and social media is that it can be difficult to determine the tone. You may mean something as a joke, but if it comes off pushy or angry, you could cause an unintended reaction from the recipient. Make sure your language is clear, and if you are angry, take a few minutes to cool down before you type. Better yet, meet in person, so nothing is misconstrued.

Table 21. SOURCE: Lindsay Olson, www.USNews.com

LINDSAY OLSON'S 10 TOP COMMUNICATION TIPS

5. Don't Be Too Casual: Getting along with your work colleagues can help you do your job better, but don't take it too far in your communication on the job. Keep the cursing for after hours, and make sure your emails, meetings, and phone calls are professional. Being too casual on the job may make others feel uncomfortable.	**6. Check Your Grammar:** Spell check is your best friend on the job. Always proofread anything you type – be it an email, tweet, or letter. If you are not great at catching errors, ask someone else to proofread it for you.
7. Keep Criticism Constructive: If you manage others, you want them to do their best. Work to ensure your comments are not emotionally charged, and that the person you are speaking with grasps what you are trying to say when giving feedback. Provide positive reinforcement when a job is well done, and find ways to add in tips for improvement without being "that boss."	**8. Restate What You Hear:** Rephrasing what your coworker or boss says to you by repeating the relevant points shows you are listening and understand what you were told. It gives both parties a chance to clarify if there is any confusion, and by repeating it, you'll remember.
9. Get A Little Personal: People let their guards down when you talk about their lives outside of work. Ask about a co-worker's kid's soccer tournament. Find ways to interact on a personal level without going too far. You will go a long way toward building trust.	**10. Never Stop Improving:** Effective communication is a skill you must practice. Observe how others respond to your communication to clue you in on areas for improvement.

Table 21. SOURCE: Lindsay Olson, www.USNews.com

***

The Art of Effective Writing

"The best writing involves an iterative process of writing, having the work criticized, and then rewriting it," says Freeman

Hrabowski, III, Ph.D., president of University of Maryland, Baltimore County. "It doesn't have to be a long communication. The most important part of writing is making sure it is well written."

In *Writing Without Bullshit!: Boost Your Career by Saying What You Mean* (Harper Business), Josh Bernoff, Ph.D. extols the value of writing clearly without hubris. The MIT-trained author identifies 10 tips for clearer writing (See: Table 22)

***

Information Technology Application

 "The illiterate of the 21ˢᵗ century will not be those who cannot read and write, but those who cannot learn, unlearn, and relearn.
— **Alvin Toffler**, Writer, Futurist

Having or not having technology skills can mean the difference between getting hired or promoted. Kristen Daniel, MBA, is CEO of Pentorship (www.Pentorship.org), a social enterprise developing products and services for organizations that train returning citizens for 21st-century careers. Daniel defines technology in its purest sense, pointing out that, "Adaptability is the core of the need for digital literacy."

"The most desirable interns or employees just know how to figure things out," she asserts.

Technological savvy is not necessarily about a particular website, software or the latest hardware.

"It is not necessary for people to become computer wizards in this new economy," she explains. "You just have to be curious and competent enough to find tools that will help you carry out tasks with very short lead times."

The Georgia Tech alumna remembers hiring an intern for a community engagement role. Despite having an undergraduate degree from a prominent public research institution and three years of professional experience, Daniel found her new worker

JEFF BERNOFF'S 10 TOP WRITING TIPS

1. BE FEARLESS: When you are afraid, you write like you are afraid. Stop hedging and say what you mean. You will get credit for directness.	2. WRITE SHORTER: Delete the warm up sentences. Organize carefully. Remove repetitive content. If you keep your emails under 250 words, people will be more likely to read them.
3. USE AN ACTIVE VOICE: Passive sentences frustrate people. Do not tell us "the new system is estimated to cost $150,000." Tell us who's responsible: "The IT department estimates that the new system will cost $150,000."	4. REVEAL STRUCTURE: Paragraphs suck for online readers, especially when stacked on one another like cinder blocks. Use headings, bullets, lists, tables, graphics, and links to make writing easier to scan and parse.
5. MANAGE REVIEWS WITH DISCIPLINE: Reviewers will ruin your best writing if you let them. Give each reviewer a specific task, like verifying technical details or grammar. Set review deadlines. Do not lose the soul of what you wrote.	6. CITE EXAMPLES: Text without examples is dull and not credible. Text with examples come alive. Spend half your time doing research.
7. USE "I," "WE," AND "YOU": These pronouns create a relationship between the writer ("I"), his organization ("we"), and the reader ("you"). Imagine the readers and write directly to them.	8. WRITE A FAT OUTLINE: Regular outlines are worthless for planning. Pretend you are writing a "treatment" for Hollywood. Include details, quotes, and ideas in your outline. Fat outlines force you to plan more thoroughly, and they are great for communicating your plan to others.
9. MOVE KEY INSIGHTS UP: You only have a few sentences to get the reader's attention. If you boldly state your key point at or near the top, they will stick around to see if you can prove it.	10. DELETE WEASEL WORDS: Every "very," "considerable," or "on the other hand" not only weakens your prose, but it also makes it longer. Get rid of qualifying words. Make specific, true statements rather than broad generalizations with qualifiers that invalidate them.

Table 22. SOURCE: www.WithoutBullshit.com

underprepared to use the many web-based applications the startup relied on to maximize its resources.

"During the onboarding process, I realized that while I spent most of my time working to expose incarcerated people to new skills, digital literacy was an issue for young people at large. In this case, the intern had the latest smartphone but had not yet learned how to use a calendar invite," recalls Daniel, a recipient of the Most Innovative Venture award from the Points of Light Foundation CivicX Accelerator Demo Night. "She was sharp, willing to learn, and enthusiastic about our mission, but beyond lifestyle applications like social media, her technology skills were lacking."

At the conclusion of the internship, Daniel had a candid discussion with her young charge. "I had to tell her that the gap between her remaining a volunteer and becoming a paid employee was her lacking the digital literacy skills that were required to fully take ownership of the role and make it what it needed to be," she remembers.

You must be able to produce desired results in the workplace regularly. It may take you using a mobile application on Monday, a cloud-based solution on Tuesday, or an entirely different tool on Wednesday to get the job done.

What matters most is your ability to produce solutions or know where to look to learn how to create the desired solution that satisfies your supervisor or client. Daniel says all employees must have a mindset that demonstrates, "I don't know this, but I will figure it out."

The Atlanta-based executive notes that acquiring technology skills can help advance your career:

> "In some organizations, senior managers might not be willing to adopt new technology or ways of handling business. Being young and technologically literate allows you to have a lot of achievement early in your career. You may be able to save your organization time and money by introducing new processes and solutions. This could help your career progress faster than ten years ago."

Daniel encourages students to start practicing and developing their tech skills now. "The first place you should start is with group assignments for courses," she advises. "Find out which platforms will allow you to collaborate with your classmates. It is the perfect gateway to professional digital literacy."

She asserts, "If you commit to using and practicing with tools that allow you to collaborate with your classmates. You will learn how to use your tech skills to save people time and you will gain project-based experience that will prepare you for the real world."

Mastering technical skills and tools like productivity software such as Microsoft Office Suite, Google's G Suite, OpenOffice.org; cloud solutions programs including OneDrive, Box, and Dropbox; collaboration solutions such as Basecamp, HipChat, and Huddle, and their respective mobile applications can help you reach your potential.

***

Leadership

66 *"If your actions inspire others to dream more, learn more, do more and become more, you are a leader."*
— **John Quincy Adams**, Sixth President of the United States 99

Joshua Fredenburg, M.A. is a leadership and diversity expert who travels the country delivering keynote addresses and workshops about various subjects. The California native defines leadership as, "The ability to influence others towards a certain action or destination." He says before you attempt to lead others, you must first lead yourself.

"Before you can lead you must have strong character and values. You must also understand your capacity and have faith to walk out your vision," says Fredenburg, author of *Are You the World's Next Top Leader.*

Lavell Crump, better known as the award-winning rapper and producer David Banner, recommends developing the ability to take responsibility and create results before seeking leadership positions.

"I look at leadership like this, it's your fault even when it's not. That's what I live by," says Banner, founder of A Banner Vision, LLC (www.ABannerVision.com), an Atlanta-based multimedia company.

Banner relays a story about his time as an ambitious upstart Hip-hop performer in Jackson, Mississippi:

> "When I first tried to be a rapper, my own family told me I couldn't make it. I could not afford beats, so I learned how to produce them myself. There was not anyone booking me, so I started renting out buildings for my shows. There is no excuse!" Banner exclaims. "I started my company with $100. I bought 100 CDs. I stood on the corner and sold them myself. I made $1,000. I took that and bought 1,000 CDs, sold them, and made $10,000. Then I bought a van and sold 10,000 more CDs. Nobody cared about Mississippi. Nobody wanted to sign a rapper from Mississippi. So I started my own company. The main thing for me is you have to do it yourself. Act as if nobody cares."

Banner said adopting the "no one cares" mindset inspired him to pursue and win election as the president of the student government association while attending Southern University in Baton Rouge. "I never wanted to be student body president. I always thought that people looking for positions like that were phony. I ran because I didn't like the way people were treating us [students]."

Celebrated neurosurgeon, Dr. Benjamin Carson shares what he calls the best advice he has received, "The person who has the most to do with what happens in your life is you. Not anybody else."

Renowned author Dr. Price Cobbs notes, "The more educated you are, the more you understand yourself, your world, where you fit in, where you don't fit in, and how to fit in."

Fredenburg, a graduate of California State University-Long Beach, recommends young scholars start taking personal inventory to evaluate their place, value, and potential. "The first step toward influencing yourself is knowing exactly who you are," he reveals. "The more I know about myself, the more I know whom I should surround myself with, and how I overcome challenges when challenges come in the way of my vision."

Fredenburg offers four fundamentals of resilient leadership:

- **IDENTIFY YOUR CONTRIBUTION:** "You must know how to use your talents and skills well. Be confident and passionate about your gift and share it with the people you intend to lead."

- **SET SMART GOALS:** "Most people think they understand this. However, setting goals and making sure you meet them is a necessary and radical part of the leadership process. Your goals must be **SMART**, meaning:

    - **S**pecific
    - **M**easurable
    - **A**ttainable
    - **R**ealistic
    - **T**imely"

- **INCREASE CAPACITY:** "You must have the capacity to get the job done in an excellent manner. If you do not currently have the capacity, find out which skills you will need to strengthen your abilities and knowledge base."

- **HAVE RESILIENT FAITH:** "Faith is the ability to act on what you believe. Resilient faith is demonstrating an ability to bounce back, ignore rejection, make adjustments, and overcome whatever challenges and obstacles that stand in between you and your desired outlook."

Employers want workers who produce high-quality results regardless of the circumstances. Organizations value employees who can inspire co-workers to do likewise. Remember, leadership is not telling people what to do. It is producing results in such a way that you attract the influence of your colleagues. Campus-based committees, clubs, and organizations offer unlimited leadership development opportunities.

***

Career Management

" *"Efforts and courage are not enough without purpose and direction."*
— **John Fitzgerald Kennedy**,
35th President of the United States "

Because the quality of your college efforts will determine your early career success and starting salaries, it is important that you use your college experience as a launching pad for your next opportunity. Your first job and salary will have a significant impact on your lifetime earning potential. Part of career management is building the soft skills, hard skills, and professional experiences to make you a compelling internship candidate or entry-level employee.

Visit and get involved in all career center offerings the minute you step on campus. Start working with a career counselor to map out a plan for the experiences you will need to compete for your top career choices.

Nearly all colleges and universities host job fairs and recruitment visits. Career centers provide professional development workshops, mock interviews, cover letter and resume review sessions, job databases, online courses, and career connection resources among other services. Joseph Thomas, director of the South Carolina State University (SCCU) Career Center, says career centers have many benefits for current students and alumni. Thomas points out:

"It's been proven that students who use career centers and participate in career center services are more likely to get hired than students who do not. We also provide the same career services to our alumni. We want our students to successfully transition from college to the world of work, but everyone must play their part. The university, the employers, and students all have a part to play. You don't want a job. You can get a job anywhere. I tell students to use this experience to launch their careers."

The longtime career services professional offers a four-part combination to unlock career success:

- **REMEMBER YOUR PURPOSE:** "Students must know their purpose and keep their goals in front of them so that they don't get distracted while they are in school."

- **BEGIN WITH THE END IN MIND:** "You have to constantly ask yourself, 'What is my end result?' and then work toward it."

- **Take College Seriously:** "College is a training facility. No employer is going to call you and make sure you are waking up early enough to show up to work on time. They are going to set standards and expect you to meet them. So, college is a great opportunity to show that you can be responsible for yourself."

- **RESPECT IS EARNED:** "If you don't take responsibility in college, you won't do it in the world of work. Once you demonstrate that you are responsible and serious about your future, it proves to your future employers that you are ready for the next level."

The "College Career Center Study" also notes 63.6 percent (roughly 13 million) of students are relying more on free and paid online services to seek career opportunities. It may help if those students had the added benefit of institutional resources and relationships with career service advocates who would champion their candidacy.

"I travel the country maintaining employer relationships," Thomas discloses. "We do career fairs, site visits, and in-class presentations to create opportunities to help our students start their careers. Own up and use these resources."

Mastering these elements will help you achieve your professional goals and make you a highly attractive candidate.

CHAPTER 11
INTERNSHIP SUCCESS
FOR THE EMERGING PROFESSIONAL

66 *"Everybody has to start somewhere. You have your whole future ahead of you. Perfection doesn't happen right away."*
— **Haruki Murakami**, Essayist, Author 99

Amantha Lott, MIS, MFA, graduated with two separate master's degrees – one in service design from the Savannah College of Arts and Design, the other in information sciences from Indiana University-Bloomington. Unlike many of her peers, Lott already accepted an employment offer from eBay before she graduated.

The Indiana native says her three internships with the San Jose-based global online marketplace gave her the inside track on a permanent offer. She initially served as a global product management intern and twice as a mobile design product management intern.

She shares that securing internships during college produced many career benefits. "It allows you to see the impact you can make as a professional. Going to class every day doesn't show you the long-term benefits of your contribution. It's amazing to create a solution and see how people benefit from your work," Lott declares.

The National Association of Colleges and Employers' 2015 survey of trends among college students revealed that employers presented at least one job offer to 72.2 percent of applicants who completed paid interns, 43.9 percent of applicants who completed unpaid interns, and only 36.5 percent of students who graduated without internship experience. Additionally, students who completed paid internships received higher starting salaries (See: Table 24).

Internships provide incredible opportunities that include exposure to future vocations, the chance to meet industry professionals, first-hand observation of career markets, and a platform to make a good impression with prospective employers. Similar to internships, cooperative education opportunities (co-ops) provide college students paid training and professional exposure.

How you perceive and act on those opportunities will have a direct impact on whether you will enjoy a successful professional career. It is not sufficient to accept just any internship in any environment just because your adviser told you to do so. It is critical that ambitious students select internships that will advance their career ambitions, enrich their professional network, and make them compelling candidates for the best employment options.

This may prompt you to ask, "How do I pick a good internship?" The answer: Become well read in your industry, be honest with yourself, and have a good idea of what you want and where you want to go. Each factor is fundamental in accomplishing your career goals.

Selecting the best internships requires a few other considerations that could influence your decision including: Knowing where you may ultimately want to live, knowing how you want to see your career progress, knowing what is a realistic starting salary for your industry, and knowing how much money you want to make after you graduate.

Pursuing an internship that is the right fit often demands you step out of your comfort zone into unfamiliar territory. Having a good idea about how your industry works will put you on the right path. The only way to start understanding how your industry functions is to consume industry data, develop relationships with industry players, and expose yourself to the industry environment.

You can find this information in industry blogs, websites, association newsletters, government reports, industry conferences, and media that serve your industry (See: Life, Liberty, and the Pursuit of an Education). You can acquire this information online, at your school library, or a local library.

Lott likens the internship experience to a romantic courtship. "You have to date a company. Internships allow you to do that by seeing the inner workings of the culture, the product life cycle, the design process, and the executive decision-making process," reveals Lott, who successfully consummated her eBay internship by converting it into a full-time service design manager position with a six-figure salary.

"The company gets to date you, too. You also get the opportunity to merge your personality with the company's culture. It's very easy to have an outside assumption of what a company is like, but until you are on the inside, you really don't know. A company that is right for your best friend might not be the right fit for you."

***

Internships: Performance Matters

Dr. Martez Prince is a licensed pharmacist and owner of Premier Pharmacy and Wellness Center based in Charlotte, North Carolina. The independent pharmacologist attributes a significant portion of his professional success to college internships. The 30-year-old entrepreneur held several internships while attending college. Dr. Prince's dedication to internships proved useful and lucrative for the community-oriented druggist.

"Every intern must make a good impression because it's a small world," Dr. Prince advises. "People talk. I encourage everyone – including interns – to manage their reputation."

He parlayed his internship experiences and a high-level of professionalism into a position as a staff pharmacist at Rite Aid Corporation. "I went there as an intern and was eventually hired as a pharmacist. When I first graduated from pharmacy school, I remember signing an offer sheet for $130,000 before bonuses and perks," recalls Dr. Prince, who says he was promoted to pharmacy manager within five months of his employment.

As a retail pharmacy owner, Dr. Prince is committed to ensuring more students have the opportunity to excel in this highly technical, well compensated, and service-oriented profession. He exercises this commitment by hiring interns, which he describes as a labor of love.

He concedes, "Managing interns is hard work. Because you have to teach them, make sure they are learning, make sure they are doing tasks correctly, and you still have to accomplish your daily tasks for the business."

Dr. Prince says he only hires interns that project three significant characteristics:

- **HAVING THE RIGHT ATTITUDE**: "Interns must be positive and show a high level of interest and passion in what they are trying to do."

- **ACTIVE ENGAGEMENT**: "I love to teach. I like for a student to ask meaningful questions. I also love when the student physically reacts to the information, gets it, and uses what they learn."

- **HIGH-LEVEL OF PROFESSIONALISM**: "Students must be on time, dressed professionally, and act professionally in the work environment. This lets me know the student is serious about this opportunity."

***

Cultivating a Plan for Internship Success

Although you want the best placement possible, the fact remains that having the right attitude, being highly engaged, and projecting yourself as a capable professional are not the only requirements to accomplishing your goals.

It is equally important to have a plan. A successful internship must be built on the foundation of a carefully thought out plan. As Benjamin Franklin put it, "If you who fail to plan, you are planning to fail." It would be helpful to draw up a professional development plan and identify your learning goals. Examine your assumptions about the internship, and then honestly ask yourself:

- How can I stand out as an intern?
- What are my expectations?
- Are my expectations realistic?
- Is there enough time to meet my learning goals and expand my understanding of my career options?

You will benefit from investing time and effort into planning and taking the necessary steps to move you closer toward your goals. Carla Harris, MBA, vice chairwoman of global wealth management and senior client adviser at Morgan Stanley, encourages students to develop a solid plan for internship and career success.

"Most people tend to think, 'well I won't get my first evaluation for a while, so I have time to show what I can do," says Harris, author of *Expect to Win: 10 Proven Strategies for Thriving in the Workplace* (Penguin Group). "You should not think that you have a long time to demonstrate what you have been hired to do, or to show that you are good at it."

In today's ultra-competitive job market, interns cannot afford to get distracted by the nervousness or excitement of a new opportunity. Harris says new hires or interns have a short period to learn the ropes and prove their worth. She points out that co-workers and supervisors, "start making informal judgments," about new hires. Those judgements can have a formal impact on that person's ability to keep their internship or earn future employment. Thus, unprepared interns are at a competitive disadvantage. The New York-based author and career coach offers insight to help you activate your three-part action plan for internship success:

- **PART I: BE PROACTIVE**: Internships require many one-to-one relationships with different people within the company, so learn the expectations as soon as possible. Just consider the possibility that by getting into the internship program in the first place means that you are working with people who are interested in helping you succeed. You'll be surprised by the number of individuals willing to share their knowledge and skills with you to promote your development. So go ahead and ask the questions. Immerse yourself into the whole working environment of the company. Harris charges interns to learn their supervisor's preferred method of communication (e.g., face-to-face, email, or memos), the company's culture, and protocol within the first two weeks of employment.

- **PART II: PERFORM**: You do not have to know everything on your first day. It is okay to feel clueless, but it is not okay to stay that way. Assumptions are not beneficial in the workplace. In Harris' second phase, she encourages interns to grow beyond impressing co-workers to maturing into a competent contributor. You can achieve this by developing various qualities such as learning how to communicate, setting and accomplishing goals; developing new skills; expanding your capacity; and being coachable and receptive to honest and helpful feedback. Many companies may offer training programs to help you establish and acquire skills. Harris suggests you secure all training programs needed to perform your tasks well within the first month on the job. She adds, "A firm may have a great training program, but it's up to you to get the training you need. You can't sit back and think somebody is going to plan it out for you."

- **PART III: PROCEED**: Employing these strategies will help you successfully navigate your work environment and effectively position you for future and better professional opportunities. The people you meet in these settings can help you secure employment. They can become your mentors, advisers, and future professional references. Harris says after their grace period, interns cannot use ignorance, inexperience, or lack of training as excuses for not performing well or not meeting expectations. She adds that within three months you should blend in and reflect the company's values. Harris asserts, "After that first quarter, you want people to forget that you are a new hire at all. You want them to feel like you've been there all along."

Harris' other book, *Strategize to Win: The New Way to Start Out, Step Up, or Start Over in Your Career* (Avery), offers even more valuable career advancement insights.

During your internships, your job is to present the best version of yourself and project impeccable professionalism. IACM designed a four-year action plan for your consideration (See: Table 23).

***

Finding the Most Desirable Companies

Knowing your preferred geographical location is another internship consideration. If you want to ultimately return to your hometown, live in a place with a moderate cost of living, or live in a new and exciting locale, it is critical that you secure at least one internship in those places. You want to try to immerse yourself in the environment before starting your career there.

IACM SELF-ASSESSMENT: When making a decision about where to launch your professional career, consider what you want your professional life to look like after you graduate. Examine both the top and median salaries for newly hired professionals in your industry (See: Paid in Full: The Price of Education). Also, assess the possible social outlets in that area.

Ask yourself the following questions:
- Do I identify with co-workers and the company culture?
- What adjustments do I have to make to succeed here?
- What would my life look like in this part of the country?

IACM INTERNSHIP ACTION PLAN

YEAR	FOCUS AREA	IDEAL LOCATION
Before Freshman Year *(Introduction)*	Securing an internship before or right after you graduate from high school gives you an exponential competitive edge. You may find yourself performing administrative and clerical tasks. Perform these tasks to the best of your ability with a grateful attitude. Your goal is to introduce yourself to future career options and develop contacts.	**Hometown or Government Opportunity**
Before Sophomore Year *(Exposure)*	Expose yourself to career options that pique your interest. Seek opportunities with companies that are known for training and development. It is also critical to develop contacts and skills that will make you attractive for future opportunities.	**Industry Advocacy and Lobby Associations; Government Opportunity; or Top Industry Firms**
Before Junior Year *(Build)*	Continue to gain experience with roles and functions you might want after graduation. Build your skill sets, contacts, communication, and cultural competencies to understand and demonstrate the language and habits needed to be successful in the workplace.	**Top Industry Firms and/or Your Desired Company**
Before or After Senior Year *(Demonstrate)*	You are on a grind and shine campaign. You want to showcase your skills to a company that is your top choice for employment. Communicate through your actions, not just your conversation, that you are capable, hungry, and ready to make a meaningful contribution to the organization. Dress, talk, and walk like one of the permanent employees. Doing so communicates you belong there!	**Your Desired Company**

Table 23.

- With whom could I develop friendships?
- Am I willing to adapt to the weather?
- Am I comfortable with the distance between my job and my family?
- Am I comfortable with the commute to work?

When choosing where you want to apply for internships, consider the NACE annual student survey that highlights sectors offering student internships. Securing a paid internship doubles the chances that you will be offered a job with a higher starting salary. (See: Table 24).

Additionally, if you are always researching your industry, you will develop an awareness of the top players in your field. You also want to know the following superlatives:

- **TOP INDUSTRY FIRMS:** Research the 10 highest performing firms in your desired industry. The top 10 companies have the largest market share (meaning they serve more people) in your industry. Internships in these environments give you access to your industry's premium performers. They expose you to your industry's best practices and professional techniques. You also get a first-hand glimpse of the culture and habits needed to perform at the highest level in your industry.

  They also tend to offer the best compensation. Internships at top-notch companies make you a highly desirable job candidate because recruiters and employers will assume you are vetted, mature, and understand the culture and demands of an ultra-competitive professional environment. You can find top industry firms in *Forbes, Fortune, Inc., BusinessWeek, Black Enterprise,* and other publications covering business news and trends.

  If you do not secure an internship directly with the company, consider the backdoor approach of applying for an internship with a company subsidiary or one of the firm's largest contractors. You can find information about the company's subsidiaries and contractors on company websites, annual reports, investor reports, federal form 990s (for nonprofit organizations), and corporate media like *CNBC, Wall Street Journal, New York Times, Crain's* publications, *Bloomberg*, and *Fox Business*.

- GOVERNMENT OPPORTUNITIES: Find out the local, state, and federal agencies and organizations that regulate your industry. Being an intern in these environments helps you develop a perspective on the types of regulations, licensing, and compliance considerations in which your industry contends. As you become familiar with various regulation cycles and the processes that allow organizations to conduct business within government standards, you are afforded the opportunity to develop

JOB OFFER RATES AND STARTING SALARIES BY INTERNSHIP/CO-OP EXPERIENCE

PAY STATUS	EMPLOYER TYPE	APPLIED	RECEIVED OFFER	OFFER RATE	MEDIAN STARTING SALARY OFFERS
PAID INTERNS	Private, For Profit Company	1,015	733	72.2 %	$52,521
	Nonprofit Organization	178	92	51.7 %	$41,876
	State or Local Government Agency	101	51	50.5 %	$42,693
	Federal Government Agency	42	26	61.9 %	$48,750
UNPAID INTERNS	Private, For Profit Company	253	111	43.9 %	$34,375
	Nonprofit Organization	299	124	41.5 %	$31,443
	State or Local Government Agency	139	47	33.8 %	$32,969
	Federal Government Agency	30	15	50 %	$42,501
NO INTERNSHIP OR CO-OP		941	343	36.5 %	$38,572

Table 24. SOURCE: NACE Class of 2015 Student Survey

connections with people who could prove helpful to your future employers.

You can find these organizations on local, state, and federal government websites and usually in the "About" section of a top company's website. Those firms tend to boast that they are ABC-certified, DEF board approved, or GHI compliant. During your internship, you want to develop relationships with people that work in the areas responsible for deadline extensions, compliance, reporting, and supporter relations. Securing contacts in these important segments will prove invaluable for your career.

Another gold mine for these types of opportunities are the state legislative, U.S. senatorial offices, or U.S. congressional committees that govern your industry. If you cannot directly serve a committee, consider serving in a committee member's office, preferably in Washington, D.C. for federal legislators. Each state Legislature has differing activity levels. Choose the most active location when deciding between either the district or Capitol Hill office.

- INDUSTRY ADVOCACY, LOBBY, AND ASSOCIATIONS: Discover the leading associations and lobby or advocacy groups for your desired industry. These opportunities introduce you to all the major players, concerns, and trends in your industry. You are exposed to the most influential participants in your industry. This friendly environment helps you understand the current challenges of your industry, the future vision of your sector, and allows you to connect with a full-spectrum of contacts in virtually every arena of your industry. Industry advocacy and associations are among the best internship opportunities because they provide access to industry firms of all sizes as well as the sector's most influential contributors. These organizations have meetings and conventions that give attendees networking opportunities and exposure to the latest industry trends. Many of these organizations will also pay you to intern at partner firms.

***

Find Organizations That Want You

Honesty and self-knowledge are crucial when searching for a high-quality work environment. If you are a woman, a member of an ethnic minority group, a current or soon-to-be parent, or a member of the Lesbian, Gay, Bisexual, Transgender, Queer, Intersex, and Asexual (LGBTQIA) community, you may want to consider investing time in researching companies that value and support these groups.

It is challenging to perform at a high level in an environment where you feel unwelcomed, bullied, or encouraged to hide who you are. Many companies value your identity, diversity, and contribution. You have to spend time looking for them, and then court, curry favor, and market yourself to those organizations. There are several valuable resources available to help find the best cultural fit for you:

- Each year in June, *Black Enterprise Magazine* produces its "B.E. 100 list of the Nation's Top Black Businesses." This resource helps you to become familiar with the highest performing Black-owned firms and mainstream companies that support and embrace the professional ambitions of Black employees. The publication also produces a list of the "Best Companies for Diversity" in an annual Diversity Issue, usually published in September.

- Each June, the Human Rights Campaign Foundation releases a "Corporate Equality Index" (CEI), which rates

American workplaces and businesses regarding lesbian, gay, bi-sexual, and transgender equality. CEI ranks companies based on having written non-discrimination policies related to sexual orientation, gender identity, and gender expression; inclusion of sexual orientation, gender identity and gender expression in its diversity and sensitivity training; parity in domestic partner benefits required by certain laws such as the Family and Medical Leave Act; appropriate and respectful advertising to the LGBTQIA community; transgender-inclusive health insurance benefits; and rejection of any activities that would undermine the goal of equal rights for LGBTQIA people. More information is available on the foundation's website at www.HRC.org.

- The National Association of Female Executives (NAFE), through its website TheWorkingMother.com, publishes several lists of family-friendly and women-friendly companies. Lists include: Best Companies for Multicultural Women, Working Mother 100 Best Companies, NAFE Top Companies for Executive Women, Top 10 Nonprofit Companies for Executive Women, and Working Mother & Flex-Time Lawyers 50 Best Law Firms for Women. This resource is particularly helpful if you have or plan to have children, or plan to expand your family. The listed companies are more likely to have benefits that support employees with kids and other family obligations.

- *Inc. Magazine* publishes a "50 Best Companies to Work" list every year. It ranks firms by employee feedback, performance innovation, workplace conditions, employee compensation, and financial security. These are important factors when considering potential jobs and internships because your first salary and first job have an impact on future wages and career opportunities.

- Social media platforms are also great resources to identify potential internship landing spots. Use your favorite search engine and periodically search for various college employment hashtags like #Intern, #Internships, #Scholarships, #JobsForStudents, #StudentJobs, #SummerInternships, or any other buzzwords associated with your interests. This helps you identify other openings.

These are just a few of the lists you will find during your research. Once you have identified a few companies, you can acquire more detailed information by reading their annual reports, company literature, and websites. Hoovers.com is another vetting resource. These companies are desirable because they are more likely to pay you competitively and give you opportunities to increase your value through professional development programs, management trainee opportunities, company exposure, skill enhancement courses, and tuition reimbursement.

***

International Assignments: Your Passport to Success

 "It's a small world after all."
— **Robert B. and Richard M. Sherman**,
Disney Songwriters

The world is so much bigger than the continental United States. Pursuing internships in another country enlarges your perspective and creates diverse professional opportunities. Omar Goff is still reaping the rewards of embarking on a 10-month college opportunity in South America.

"Interning abroad broadened my worldview and gave me a competitive advantage over my peers," Goff says of his Sao Paulo, Brazil-based college internship with Pfizer, a leading international biopharmaceutical company. "Brazil was the world's hottest economy at that time. Now, I can say that I worked and thrived there. I believe it will give me a competitive advantage over the long-term."

This experience was invaluable five years later when an international opportunity at a Procter and Gamble (P&G) Brazil operations site became available. "I became the prime candidate because I worked in the market," reveals Goff, who currently works as a brand manager for P&G's Old Spice brand.

Working in a foreign country also increased his compensation. "I enjoyed a very comfortable lifestyle due to the expatriate compensation. I was able to accumulate significant savings, eliminate significant debt, and enjoy life. It was quite lucrative for me."

Goff says there were personal benefits as well. "People invited me into their homes and became my family. My ability to communicate with others enhanced my social life because I was able to talk to people. I built lifelong relationships while I was in Brazil."

You can also cash in by choosing the right country. Several economists and business leaders have identified Brazil, Russia, India, and China as the emerging markets for business opportunities and investment. *Fortune Magazine* recently added The Republic of Colombia, Indonesia, Kenya, Malaysia, Mexico, Poland, and the United States to the list of promising markets (See: Table 25).

Learning an official language or pursuing professional opportunities in these designated countries would benefit any student. Visit your school's honors program, international exchange program, and study abroad program to explore opportunities to travel the globe.

***

You STILL Have More Work to Do

66 *"Work, work, work, work, work, work."*
— **Rihanna**, Grammy Award-Winning Singer 99

After all of those efforts, there is still more work to do. Yes, more work. If you want to take your internship to the next level, you cannot just work your job. You have to work your city and region as well. The alumni association in your town is a treasure trove of valuable contacts and resources. Contemplate how much you can gain from fellow alumni.

TOP GLOBAL ECONOMIES			
Country	Most Popular Language	Population (Millions)	+Gross National Product (Trillions)
China	Mandarin	1,367	$19.39
USA	English	321	$17.95
India	Hindi (41 percent)	1,251	$7.965
Russia	Russian	142	$3.7
Brazil	Portuguese	204	$3.19
Indonesia	Bahasa Indonesia	255	$2.842
Mexico	Spanish	121.7	$2.2
Poland	Polish	38.5	$1
Columbia	Spanish	46.7	$0.667
Malaysia	Bahasa Malaysia	30.5	$0.296
Kenya	English	45	$0.141

Table 25. SOURCE: *The World Fact Book*, Central Intelligence Agency, Estimates 2015. Numbers were converted to U.S. currency. The countries were sourced by the Fortune website.

Volunteer with the local alumni chapter. Schedule an appointment with your university's alumni affairs coordinator and your clubs and organizations coordinator to help connect with fellow members in your city. You can also use social media platforms like LinkedIn and Facebook to locate them on your own.

"During your internship, you get to meet some incredibly smart people. I've worked with people that have had significant accomplishments like securing patents, earning Ph.Ds., and even some who have delivered presentations at the White House," Lott informs. "I've made some of my best friends during my internship experience. Outside of work, I met a sorority sister in San Jose. She helped me negotiate my employment offer with eBay."

The only way to expand your network is to put your feet on the pavement, introduce yourself to everyone, and strategically communicate your interests and ambitions.

The greatest asset you have to offer while you are interning is a positive attitude, a respectful demeanor, and your eager willingness to volunteer. Yes, volunteer, for FREE! You can fold programs, set up meeting spaces, clean up event space, build websites, pass out drinks, use social media to promote those events, pass out flyers, and do whatever is ethically and spiritually sound to make connections that will advance your career.

You may also consider volunteering with the local chapters of professional and interest groups in your city. Also, attend networking events hosted by local politicians and chambers of commerce. You must have a presence in all these areas because they are treasure houses of industry gossip (trends, players, and developments), potential opportunities, professional information, local insight, and professional relationships.

***

The 14 Commandments for College Interns

There are many unspoken rules regarding internships that help people become successful. It is important to understand that your job as an intern is to be a good student and to do your part to make the experience as professional and pleasurable as possible. Some unspoken rules include not seeking additional face time with your supervisor, not wasting your supervisor's time, not using your cell phone or company phones for unnecessary personal calls, or having people repeat things they already told you. IACM produced 14 Commandments to help students navigate the professional ebb-and-flow of the workplace. They include:

IACM'S 14 COMMANDMENTS FOR COLLEGE INTERNS

1. Interns shall never be late. In fact, interns shall arrive at least 10 minutes early and stay later.
2. Interns shall have an incredible work ethic. They shall also find ways to perform well and contribute to the organization, (e.g., volunteering on company initiatives and social projects, etc.)
3. Interns shall be proactive. They will schedule standing 1-on-1's with managers and core team members, report results, and track their work progress, etc.
4. Interns shall not struggle with assignments in silence. They will leverage other resources (i.e., other interns, co-workers, and alumni) before engaging their direct manager. Interns shall network with a purpose and attend every company-affiliated event or gathering when invited.
5. Interns shall be coachable, regularly ask for feedback, and immediately implement said feedback. They will not wait until the end of the internship.
6. Interns shall write down all assignments and repeat said duties to the supervisor before leaving to work on assigned tasks earnestly.
7. Interns shall master their current role before seeking expanded responsibilities.
8. Interns shall be overly prepared. In fact, interns will discreetly have an extra copy of important items in case the supervisor or essential personnel leaves their copy behind.
9. Interns shall not be caught socializing or using personal communication devices while on the clock.

10. Interns shall not ask un-job-related personal questions of co-workers, company employees, or supervisors.
11. Interns shall NEVER, EVER gossip. EVER!
12. Interns shall NEVER complain about their supervisor or work environment to anyone affiliated with the company, unless it is related to workplace harassment.
13. Interns shall NOT fraternize (sexually) with co-workers or fellow interns.
14. Interns shall respect the established chain of command and organization protocol.

CHAPTER 12
DIVERSITY: OWNING YOUR PERSONAL POWER

> " *Success is liking yourself, liking what you do, and liking how you do it.* "
> — **Maya Angelou**, Poet, Humanitarian "

The world market is globalizing at a rapid pace. Many of the world's leading firms are making efforts to cultivate work climates that reflect the full spectrum of humanity including race, gender, sexuality, religion, age, geographic location, and cultural identities.

To be fair, diversity and inclusion is a vague concept from a corporate standpoint, so everyone (interns, employees, and organizations) is still in a learning, trial-and-error phase. Numerous firms are investing in the capacity to create benchmarks and strategies to enhance inclusion through procurement, employment, and governance. Despite the market's best efforts to meet the demands of inclusion and diversity, there are still occasions where some people feel unwelcome.

Marie McKenzie, MIB, an executive within the travel and tourism industry, says people can overcome professional challenges by tapping into their personal power. "I enter a room believing that I belong there. I also go with the belief that my input is just as valuable, if not more valuable, than my peers," declares McKenzie, vice president of global destinations services and sourcing at Carnival Corporation, PLC, the world's largest travel and leisure company.

Personal power is knowing that you can make a contribution to your organization. It is also making a personal commitment to having direct and open communication, defined goals, mutual respect and trust, keeping your word, consistently adding value to your company and colleagues. Additionally, it includes maintaining your personal integrity and company ethics.

When you build your own power, you present your very best work regardless of the circumstances. Your work and essence become a product of love that reflects who you are and how you represent yourself; not a product based on fear and doubts.

McKenzie suggests reimagining your differences and uniqueness as strengths and not weaknesses. She reveals, "I go into the room with my talent and my experience. I sell myself on that. That's what my focus is. I advise everyone to never go to the table focusing on the fact that you are a minority or a woman."

McKenzie started her career with Arthur Andersen, LLP in Washington, D.C. She arrived at Carnival Cruise Lines in 1996 as a senior staff auditor. In less than two years, she was promoted to revenue accounting manager. Throughout her tenure, she served in various capacities with growing responsibilities at both the Carnival Cruise Lines brand and its parent company Carnival Corp. She earned promotions in the midst of market fluctuations, international economic challenges, and management changes. She accomplished this all while simultaneously earning a master's degree in international business from Florida International University.

In her role, McKenzie's global responsibilities include growing Carnival Corporation's assets and creating exciting customer experiences. She also leads a team of brand experts responsible for geographical regions on behalf of all nine of Carnival's brands: Carnival Cruise Line, Holland America Line, Princess Cruises, Seabourn, Cunard, AIDA Cruises, Costa Cruises, P&O Cruises (Australia), and P&O Cruises (United Kingdom). The Jamaica native encourages emerging professionals to focus on presenting solutions in the workplace.

"I find that when you present yourself like that, you have more success. If what you have to say is a fact or a strongly supported opinion, it cannot be disputed," she advises. The Howard University alumna says focusing on yourself as a minority puts you at a competitive disadvantage. "I am the only me ever made. That exclusivity gives me power," McKenzie asserts.

Use your power to accomplish your goals.

CHAPTER 13
NETWORKING 101

> ❝ *"It takes teamwork to make the dream work. Your network is your net worth!"*
> — **George C. Fraser**, Author, Networking Expert ❞

You can probably finish this statement: "It isn't what you know. It's _____ you know!" That's right! "It's who you know." Chasity Echols-Brown, Ed.D., learned the value of getting to know people as she was preparing to graduate from Florida Memorial University (FMU) without any job prospects.

> "My soror found out I didn't have a job and introduced me to a fellow sorority sister who was also a high school principal at the time. She hired me on the spot because I was a graduating member of Delta Sigma Theta, Inc. in need of a job. Having a soror as my mentor was very important. I did not know how to be an educator, because my degree was in business, not education. She really helped me with understanding and developing my teaching and classroom management skills. She connected me with other Deltas at the school. They supported me through the ups and downs of teaching at an inner city school. I was 22-years-old and my students were close to my age."

After three years, Dr. Echols-Brown realized the classroom was not the best setting for her. She decided to tap into her network once again to find a better professional fit. "I talked to then- (FMU School of Education) Dean Mildred Berry, Ed.D., and Ms. Alexander at FMU. They told me about the school's new one-year accelerated educational master's program (M.Ed.)," she says. "I was able to take advantage of the program and earn my master's degree for free."

After graduating with her master's degree in Exceptional Education/ESOL, Dr. Echols-Brown entered an accelerated program that helped educators become administrators. With the recommendation of her new principal and sponsorship from yet another sorority sister, Dr. Echols-Brown successfully transitioned into an assistant principal position at Booker T. Washington Senior High School at age 26, four years after she was first hired. She credits a significant portion of her professional success to her relationships and networking.

Dr. Echols-Brown advises:

> "If nobody knows you, you will not get the job ... Being connected with my sorority and college definitely helped my career. Networking can make or break your career. I know so many fellow students who went to school with me that thought all they had to do was pass their classes and go home. Now, these same people are looking to connect with people with clout and influence to help them get to the next level in their careers. At Booker T. Washington, I was younger than many of my colleagues. However, with the benefit of networking and getting my credentials, I was able to get promoted and become their boss. So, be kind and connect with everybody."

People generally like doing business with people they know, like, and trust. It is a not-so-well-kept secret that most people hired for jobs are referred by someone they know. College is a great place to either start or continue the lifelong process of getting to know people and developing the life-enriching skill of relationship management. Whether you believe it or not, you have a network. Your network is all the people you both ask for help and to whom you lend your help.

"My general rule of networking is that you never ask anyone for favors unless you have added value to them first," consults George C. Fraser, president and CEO of FraserNet, a professional development and networking firm. "Networking begins with serving first and asking later."

Your network includes everyone you know. It could be your professor, fraternity brother or sorority sister, or the church member that gives you a ride to the grocery store. This network helps increase your quality of life and your ability to succeed. This definition begs the question: Is your network pushing you toward or pulling you away from your goals?

"As your network grows, you grow," Fraser informs.

Think about how much you have gained from other people. In college, you have a built-in network of classmates, alumni, professors, advisers, faculty, and staff members at your disposal, so marshal your courage, organize, and optimize this network for your collective success, benefiting both you and the people in your network. Fraser asserts, "You cannot reach your dreams by yourself. There is no success that you can maintain and sustain on your own."

Your educational, personal, and professional success is directly connected to the people with whom you spend the most time. You will eventually mimic their habits, good, or bad. If you want to accomplish your goals, you have to reach out to people that can help you complete the task(s).

Sometimes you meet a person. Other times you just click with someone. Clicking is a feeling that signals the start of a mutually beneficial relationship. It is a spirit that is needed to produce great results. In his book *Click: 10 Truths to Creating Extraordinary Relationships* (McGraw-Hill), Fraser recommends cultivating a network that challenges you to propel to higher levels of success.

"If you're the smartest person in your network," Fraser says, "you're in the wrong darn network." The former Fortune 500 administrator recommends developing a three-pronged personal, operational, and strategic network.

***

Building a Personal Network

Fraser describes a personal network as a circle of friends who support and cheer you on. These people recharge your battery and help you sort out personal and emotional challenges. Their encouragement helps you to do your best.

You may consider your personal network your family, friends, and fellow students at your school and other institutions. They love you whether you are up or down. You give and receive unconditional love that supports you through your failures and helps you celebrate your successes. From the day you walk on campus until the day you walk across the stage to receive your hard-earned degree, you must adopt a mission to connect with the right peers. Connect wisely!

Sampson Davis, M.D., grew up in a crime-riddled, under-resourced Newark, New Jersey community. Despite being a relatively good kid, a teenaged Dr. Davis served time in a juvenile detention center for a botched robbery. He realized he was blessed to overcome his youthful mistake. Dr. Davis leveraged his personal network to accomplish his dreams.

> "There were three of us: myself, Rameck Hunt, and George Jenkins. We realized like Malcolm X said, that education was the passport to our future. We made a pact to get out of our tough neighborhood. One day in high school, we decided to skip class and play basketball instead, but we were confronted by a security guard. We knew he would ask us for a hall pass. We did not have one. He gave chase, so we ran from him toward the gym, but before we could get to the gym the principal was in front of the door and started walking toward us. The only escape was an open door to the school library."

Unbeknownst to the mischievous trio, Stetson University was hosting an informational session for its Pre-Medicine/Pre-Dental Plus program specifically designed to encourage minority students to pursue medical careers. The program also offered financial support.

"We stayed the entire hour and afterward George was excited. He said, 'Hey, this is what we are going to do. We will all become doctors.' I was considering business as a career, but I liked the fact that we would be doing this together."

They were all accepted into the program. Their bond helped encourage the first-generation college students through the challenges and fluctuations of their rigorous programs.

> "George, Rameck, and I were able to depend on each other. All of us grew up without our fathers. We learned how to be men from each other. It was absolutely priceless to have a group of my oldest and closest friends going through the process with me. We stumbled upon something special. We came from broken homes and communities. We had violence and drugs in our families. None of us thought we could become doctors at first. We stuck it out. Miracles can happen when you work hard, dig deep, and roll up your bootstraps."

Four years later, Davis and Hunt realized their goals when they graduated with Doctor of Medicine (M.D.) degrees from Robert Wood Johnson Medical School in New Brunswick, New Jersey. Back in Newark, Jenkins fulfilled his promise and graduated from the University of Medicine and Dentistry of New Jersey with a Doctor of Medical Dentistry (DMD) degree. Their story was highlighted in several media outlets including the *New York Times* bestselling *The Pact: Three Young Men Make a Promise and Fulfill a Dream* (Riverhead Books), "The PACT" documentary (WGBH Video) and on www. ThreeDoctors.com.

The service-oriented trio founded the Three Doctors Foundation, Inc. to promote educational excellence around the country. Dr. Davis prescribes a four-part plan for building a powerful personal network:

- **WORK ON YOURSELF:** "Everything starts with you. You have to be honest, be dedicated, and take care of your own business."

- **FIND LIKE-MINDED PEOPLE:** "Once you are ready to work, then you can find other people that are trying to go where you want to go."

- **SHOW UP AND BE ACCOUNTABLE:** "We had each other's back. I had to make sure I showed up and delivered my part. We all had that responsibility, so we didn't have to check each other. We all had a role to play."

- **STICK TOGETHER AND GET TO WORK:** "We never let hate or jealousy come between us. If there was a scholarship opportunity out there and we had to read a 1,000-page book, we'd each read 333 pages accordingly. We worked together to better ourselves."

Dr. Davis is a board-certified emergency medicine physician. He recently wrote *Living and Dying in Brick City: an E.R. Doctor Returns Home* (Random House).

His success proves that you have to filter out the slackers and haters. You cannot allow anyone or anything to hold your future hostage. It may sound harsh, but you are spending too much money, time, and energy on your education to waste it on people who are not serious. In college, you have to develop the ability to consistently advance your self-interest and remain stubbornly focused. You cannot allow loafers to bring you down. The best way to help someone is to lead by example. Show them better than you can tell them.

Connect with serious students. These are pupils who are studious and focused on performing at a high level, graduating from school, and getting to the next step in their journey. Do not allow others to make you responsible for their education. These are the idlers that say, "Why didn't you remind me to turn in that paper," or "You are too serious. Let's have fun and do the homework later."

You can figure out the serious students by observing the leading voices in your classes. If a student is excelling in class, always asking questions, and has good attendance, that may make him/her a prime candidate for your network. However, do not be a drag on that person. Seek to develop a mutually beneficial partnership. Remember, Fraser's premium rule for networking is everyone must add value.

***

Cultivating an Operational Network

Fraser describes the operational network as people you work with and with whom you do business. He points out that, "These are people who help you achieve certain goals."

You can consider these people your associates, peers, and people with whom you conduct business. You can depend on them to help you professionally.

Since he was in high school, Mashaun Simon, M.Div., has been building an operational network because he "needed someone to go to for guidance."

During college, Simon joined the Atlanta Association of Black Journalists, a local chapter of the National Association of Black Journalists (NABJ), a national networking and professional development association serving Black journalists. Simon was able to develop relationships with several mentors, fellow college students, and colleagues. He then leveraged their relationships, guidance, and insight into professional opportunities. NABJ also provided him a brain trust of comrades and experienced professionals he could trust during tough times.

> "It gave me this opportunity to see and interact with other professionals in the journalism space. I was able to develop relationships with them and talk to them about things that I thought I might like to do. I would bounce these ideas off of my mentor, Keith Reed, and he would say, 'Mashaun, go talk to this person.' That was very helpful. All of my internships, except one, came through NABJ.
>
> It was because I connected with these people that I got the guidance to make myself competitive for internships and job opportunities. I could bounce story ideas off of them. If I was ever at a roadblock, I could call them and

get ideas on how to approach a story or we might often give each other heads ups on job opportunities.

Because of the relationships I built with people over the years, I have been able to consistently freelance with media outlets. Through the years, I have had to reciprocate by giving back to my colleagues as well. It is critical to respect people's reputations. You never want to make a person look bad because they gave you a shot."

Simon was able to secure internships and jobs at respected media outlets including *Black Enterprise, The Atlanta Daily World, Atlanta Journal Constitution,* and *theGrio.com.* Simon continues to benefit from seeds planted in college during his reign as NABJ's student representative.

Simon offers an effective combination for putting power into your operational network:

- **UNDERSTAND THE POWER OF CONNECTION:** "Connect with everybody, not just faculty and staff. Having relationships makes it easier to ask for help. After my first year in grad school, I built a relationship with people in the financial aid and registration departments. I was telling one of the staff members that I was having a problem with my adviser and didn't know what to do. She then said, 'You know you can change your adviser, right?' That advice was critical because I would not have known otherwise. If you are not able to successfully connect with the people on your campus, I do not know how you will end up being successful."

- **UNDERSTAND THE POWER OF PRESENCE:** "I applied for seminary, but deferred that acceptance for a year. There was a running joke about me because I kept coming to the school's first Tuesday dinner for incoming students, despite not being enrolled, but I understood the power of presence. With me transitioning from journalism to theology, it was important for me to start building relationships and understanding the campus. Being present and connected assisted me in being a better student on my end."

***

Creating a Strategic Network

Fraser defines a strategic network as, "people you look up to like your mentors, role models, and coaches. They drag you into the 21st century. They are smarter than you. Their guidance takes you to the next level."

Morgan Stanley executive Carla Harris advises students to start recruiting sponsors, mentors, and advisers to help them achieve current and future success. You can find these key people at your school, internships, professional organizations, and in everyday life. The high finance expert offers this blueprint for career success.

"You must understand who the players are. Identify the decision makers, the collaborators, and the people who make things happen, and connect with them," Harris advises.

The double Harvard graduate encourages emerging professionals to take a proactive approach when recruiting their advisers, mentors, and sponsors because these key people are not always likely to reach out to you.

She adds, "In some cases, these people may be attracted to you, but it's rare that a person will connect with you and volunteer to help you move up the ladder. You have to seek them out and recruit them!"

Harris explains that advisers are people you ask for specific information that helps you navigate the college or workplace terrain. Advisers also help you define the landscape.

"An adviser is someone who can help you in your early days in the organization," she informs. "You can ask them direct and discreet information to help you advance in the organization. For example, you may ask an adviser to introduce you to a future collaborator, or you may ask them for information about a presentation you've never done before."

Harris says a mentor is an experienced person who knows you very well. You can tell them the good, the bad, and the ugly. She reveals that you can be authentic with this person.

"A mentor must be someone you can trust. They know your context. They understand the business model and can help you along the way," she shares. "They help you navigate and strategize about what's next for your career."

The Wall Street investment banker defines a sponsor as a person who spends their political capital on you. Sponsors help you obtain a desirable set of opportunities like salaries, promotions, and high value projects. They have clout, credibility, influence, and can advocate for your advancement.

"A sponsor must have capital (influence) and must be interested in spending it on you," Harris adds. "Once you identify a potential sponsor, you have to begin to develop a relationship with them and expose them to your work because it is very hard for a person to advocate for you if they can't credibly speak about your work and the value you add to the organization."

Additionally, Harris says, "You can survive a long time in your career without a mentor, but you will not move upward in any organization without a sponsor."

Lastly, Harris says employees must understand which qualities and characteristics make them a good candidate for their desired job. After identifying those qualities, she urges students to practice, master, and demonstrate them.

Harris is a sought after career expert and comments in various media about career development and advancement. Find out more at www.CarlasPearls.com.

***

Managing Your Relationships

Nobody wants to be used, so your networks must benefit everyone involved. Service to others and sharing resources are the glue that holds networks together. Periodically reach out to people in your network. You can text, email, or send a card at least once every three months. Call or visit them at least twice a year.

It is a full-time job making your dreams happen. Use these three effective ways to maintain your presence and relationships with your business contacts. You must consistently engage these people to create unlimited college, career, and life success.

***

Best Ways to Maintain Your Network

- **USE HOLIDAYS:** This can be tricky because some people, for various reasons, do not celebrate holidays. Holidays tend to be a slower and more relaxed time in some professional environments. New Year's Day is a great neutral opportunity to reach out to your network. Congratulate contacts on the year they had and wish them a more prosperous one. You can also use Veterans Day and/or Memorial Day if they or their close loved ones had served or were military casualties. Remember, Veterans Day is for honoring people who served in the Armed Forces. Memorial Day commemorates soldiers who died in service.

- **USE TECHNOLOGY:** Keep up with the triumphs, trials, and happenings of your network with Google Alerts (www.google.com/alerts). This free resource will help you stay aware of special events in their lives. Send an encouraging card or email if someone is going through a trial or death of a loved one. Send a congratulatory email or card if someone won an award or locked down a substantial piece of business. Use your Twitter or Facebook accounts to share stories about their successes with your community. You should always text, call, or email them with your congratulations. Utilizing professional social networking sites like LinkedIn also helps you stay in touch and make people aware of your professional progress.

- **HOST AN EVENT:** Host a get-together, happy hour, or festive event to bring your network together to socialize and catch up. It can be a Super Bowl party, Mid-term Mixer, or Tax Day lunch.

***

HELP!! It is Okay to Ask for Assistance

Many times the difference between whether students graduate on time or whether they graduate at all is their willingness to ask to for help. Several education studies note that female students are more likely than their male counterparts to seek help. Thus, they enjoy the benefits of receiving the necessary assistance. Dr. Barbara Inman, a career education administrator, says there is no justification for not getting the help you need to succeed in college.

"A student may not want to appear to need help," says Dr. Inman, vice president of Administrative Services and Student Affairs at Hampton University. "They must get over that. No one is proficient in everything. We can all learn something every day."

Student Affairs departments are filled with paid staff members dedicated to helping students successfully navigate their college experience. Despite this fact, Dr. Inman says she would like to see more young people take advantage of the resources.

"Students must develop a drive and passion for doing well and have a mindset that they are going to be successful," she adds. "Once they develop that mindset, they will be willing to do whatever it takes to be successful in college."

The Hampton alumna says there are no excuses for not reaching out for help. "Students must take the initiative to recognize their strengths and understand where they may need some assistance," proclaims Dr. Inman, a doctoral graduate of the University of Delaware. "It is important that students begin to identify the resources at their institution that might be helpful."

FOUR MUST HAVE RESOURCES FOR EFFECTIVE NETWORKING	
An Elevator Speech	It is helpful to craft a brief introduction that allows you to introduce yourself, highlight your interests, showcase your accomplishments, and impress contacts. Your elevator speech should be no more than 30 seconds. You can learn how to create an elevator speech at www.IAmCollegeMaterial.com.
Business Card	The old school business card still makes a good impression. Have a professionally designed business card that features your name, phone number, e-mail, major and projected graduation date. BONUS: It would also be helpful if you have a savvy tagline that showcased your career interest. Examples: Aspiring Pharmacist or Future Dentist. You can find affordable designers at www.Fiverr.com and have the cards printed at your local office supply store or copy center.
Social Media Profiles	Develop a Facebook, Twitter, and LinkedIn profile that projects you as a professional and desirable candidate. Connect with contacts via your social media sites.
Camera Phone	Use your camera phone to capture and share pictures. These pictures come in handy when you meet contacts. When you send electronic communications, you can attach these photos to remind the contact who you are and where you met.
Relentless Follow-Up	So many people go to various events and collect business cards. Few people follow-up. You can easily separate yourself from the crowd by having integrity, delivering on your promises, and following up with a thank you card or e-mail as appropriate.

Table 26.

Student Affairs divisions are usually the school's largest non-academic department. In most instances, student discipline, chaplain, housing, career center, health centers, intramural sports, student counseling, student support services, scholarship coordinators, and other student-centered components services fall under the division. She reiterates that students need to make certain they seek out that assistance.

Dr. Inman advises students to, "Start with the end in mind. The ultimate goal is to graduate from school and transition into graduate school or a job."

The university executive charges undergraduates to challenge themselves to build relationships if they want to successfully transition to their next opportunity. "To get your dream job or dream graduate school, you must develop relationships around the entire school," she says. "Students must tell themselves that in order to get my dream job or dream graduate school, I have to eventually get recommendation letters and referrals from people at my school."

Dr. Freeman Hrabowski, III, who has served as president of the University of Maryland-Baltimore County (UMBC) since 1992, agrees with Dr. Inman. "It starts with students developing the confidence to ask for help," notes Dr. Hrabowski, author of several books including *Holding Fast to Dreams: Empowering Youth from the Civil Rights Crusade to STEM Achievement* (Beacon Press).

"Students have to understand the type of help they need and identify the right people to help them. Students should have a 'Kitchen Cabinet' – a go-to support network – to assist them throughout college," Dr. Hrabowski advises.

IACM'S 10 MUST-HAVE RELATIONSHIPS FOR COLLEGE STUDENTS

1. **FELLOW STUDENTS:** You want to develop a likable and approachable persona during your time on campus. Your peers should see you as a positive, authentic, and competent person. These students will eventually become your colleagues, valuable contacts, and people who can help you achieve certain tasks both now and in the future. The Student Government Association, student

clubs and organizations, housing mates, and daily classes offer great opportunities to connect with other students. To gain helpful insight into the collegiate landscape, education champion Dr. Jawanzaa Kunjufu recommends students pursue relationships with upperclassmen who have the same career ambitions. IACM RECOMMENDATION: **Seek these relationships as soon as you step on campus and continue developing them on an ongoing basis**.

2. **ACADEMIC ADVISER:** Academic advisers are critical allies during your matriculation. Advisers help you enroll in the best classes and make sure you are on the right path to graduation. You can converse with your adviser about alternative classes. For example, they may suggest you enroll in an Analysis of Functions class instead of Calculus to satisfy your math requirements. They can help you advocate for favorable courses and they counsel you about the best practices for course and curriculum management. This person is typically a staff or faculty member employed by your school within the institution. They are also your sounding board on all of your academic concerns. IACM RECOMMENDATION: **Seek this relationship as soon as you step on campus.**

3. **INFLUENTIAL PROFESSOR(S):** Observe the political terrain at your school and begin to recruit teachers who can help you along your educational journey. This person can help you position yourself for the intra-school opportunities and maximize your college experience. This person can introduce you to other influential people at your institution and in their network. You can build a meaningful relationship by performing well academically, volunteering and supporting things that are of interest to them, and respecting the professional distance required to maintain workplace decorum. IACM RECOMMENDATION: **Seek this relationship once you are officially within your major.**

4. **HOUSING DEPARTMENT STAFF:** this department is responsible for all university-based student housing. Having favorable relations and rapport with department staff can help you secure favorable housing assignments. You can build a meaningful relationship by staying in touch with employees (electronically and in-person), volunteering at their events, and posting flyers and social media posts about housing information and news. <u>IACM RECOMMENDATION</u>: **Seek these relationships as soon as you step on campus and continue developing them on an as needed basis**.

5. **CAREER CENTER STAFF:** The career center is your school's primary contact for job and internship prospects. Each year, career centers host job fairs, professional development workshops, resume' and cover letter reviews, mock interviews, and recruiter visits, among other services. Developing connections can get you first dibs on upcoming professional opportunities. You can cement your relations with staff by volunteering to staff job fairs, create packets, pass out fliers, and spread the word about the center's services and events. As you develop a reliable presence, you will be among the first candidates on their minds when they need to identify prospects for recruiters. Your school (academic major) may also have a career or internship liaison. You must develop a relationship with them as well. <u>IACM RECOMMENDATION</u>: **Seek this relationship as soon as you step on campus.**

6. **OFFICE OF ALUMNI AFFAIRS:** The alumni affairs office is a great resource that connects the university with its alumni. On many campuses, the alumni association president is a member of the college's Board of Trustees. If you want to network with influential graduates or former students in your field, the alumni affairs staff can help you make that connection. Also, join your school's pre-alumni organization, if it has one. <u>IACM</u>

RECOMMENDATION: **Seek this relationship by the first semester of your junior year.**

7. OFFICE OF STUDENT AFFAIRS: Student Affairs is a large division. Developing staff relationships can have a positive impact on virtually every aspect of the student life outside of academics. Connections in this office can help you develop favorable results should you have a housing issue, student discipline concerns, spiritual questions, or find yourself looking for jobs, internships, and scholarships. IACM RECOMMENDATION: **Seek this relationship as soon as you step on campus.**

8. OFFICE OF THE DEPARTMENT CHAIRPERSON: The department chairperson is the highest administrator within your academic major unit. Chairs manage the concerns and affairs of students, faculty and staff members within your section. This person often serves the section's interests and helps create policies that impact the division and school. Many times the chairperson can override courses so you can get into closed classes. At most institutions, the chair signs your graduation application before it goes to the dean and eventually the provost. A connection with your chairperson could prove valuable throughout your college experience. IACM RECOMMENDATION: **Seek this relationship by the second semester of your sophomore year.**

9. OFFICE OF THE DEAN OF YOUR PROGRAM: The dean is the senior executive in your school. Every department's staff and faculty member answers to the dean, who has final say on the school's policies, procedures, and budget. They often use some of that budget to help students attend professional conferences, secure educational resources, and bring in experts to address the school. Often, he or she has a direct relationship with recruiters that seek to hire students for jobs and internships. The dean often chairs the school's intra-scholarships

committees. Having a rapport with your dean is an invaluable asset throughout your college and professional career. IACM RECOMMENDATION: **Seek this relationship by the second semester of your junior year.**

10. **OFFICE OF THE PRESIDENT:** It is unrealistic to expect to have a traditional relationship with a university president. The president is busy handling the demands of their job and finding resources for the school. You want to develop a friendly and professional rapport with an influential member of the president's office. You can achieve this by introducing yourself and offering to volunteer for any on-campus and local off-campus events sponsored by the president's office. You can also ask for a copy of the president's local calendar and show up to off-campus events the president attends on behalf of the institution. Make sure you greet and shake hands with them after they deliver speeches and lead campus events. This helps you develop a professional rapport and demonstrates that you support the president and your institution. IACM RECOMMENDATION: **Seek this relationship by your junior year.**

***

Creating Your Kitchen Cabinet

UNCF's Dr. Michael Lomax says one of the biggest myths he has encountered during his career in education is, "students thinking someone else is going to help them along." The former Dillard University president notes, "College is different from K-12. It is a different experience."

Dr. Lomax tells students to commit to making the necessary adjustments to graduate and transition into an exciting future. He also says do not take for granted the people that can help you.

"I do want students to seek guidance, support, and help, but the Lord helps those who help themselves. They have to assume some responsibility," adds Dr. Lomax, a former Fulton County Board of Commissioners chairman. "Students have to accommodate and make adjustments for their college experience. Expect that things are going to be different. They have to understand those differences and navigate their way through them. Schools have guidance and support systems, but students have to seek them out."

UMBC President Hrabowski encourages pupils to start building relationships before they need them. He counsels students to observe, learn, and employ effective ways to connect with these contacts.

"Students must understand that there are some rules of the game about speaking, dressing, and interacting with people that will help them to get ahead," Dr. Hrabowski emphasizes. "It's not a matter of them not being able to say or dress how they want. It's about doing what will help them get ahead and get the support they need."

IACM highlights seven tools to help you develop relationships with faculty and staff members:

- **WRITE A WELL-WRITTEN INTRODUCTION EMAIL OR LETTER:** President Hrabowski advises students first to introduce themselves to a particular faculty or staff member by sending a well-written letter or e-mail. He warns, "The letter should be brief, no more than three paragraphs, and well-written." The UMBC chief says a poorly written letter negatively reflects on the writer and will not get taken seriously. He summarizes, "Tell them your name, where you are coming from, and your desire to schedule an appointment with them about a particular need you may have."

- **FOLLOW UP WITHIN A WEEK:** Dr. Hrabowski encourages students to call the contact a week later. He says you cannot depend on an e-mail to cement the connection. He explains, "The email just works to get people thinking about you." He emphasizes that your goal should be to secure a face-to-face meeting.

- **SHOW UP POSITIVE AND PROFESSIONAL:** Dr. Hrabowski encourages students to have an upbeat attitude and smile during their meeting. He advises students to dress appropriately. The longtime president notes, "That doesn't necessarily mean suit and tie, but you want to dress in a way that communicates that you are meeting with someone who is important." Dr. Hrabowski says the old fashion way still helps. He continues, "It can be off-putting to people if students don't take a little time to make sure they look presentable."

- **COMMUNICATE YOUR INTERESTS CLEARLY:** Hampton University Vice President Inman urges students to be clear and direct about the purpose of the meeting. She says, "Let them know you are interested in a service they provide. Then, ask them to tell you a little more about it."

- **SEND A THANK YOU NOTE:** Sending a thank you card after a first meeting will show gratitude to your contact and help you stand out.

- **FOLLOW UP AGAIN:** If you went to a contact for advice or as a resource, make sure you send a follow-up email with the result of their input or connection. For example, if your academic adviser connected you with Mr. Smith, the campus career counselor who helped you secure an internship, write your adviser to express thanks for the connection. Provide brief detail about what happened and the results. This both extends the experience for the adviser and keeps them informed about your dealings.

- **VOLUNTEER:** Volunteering and supporting your contacts' initiatives and projects can help you develop productive relationships. Dr. Inman reminds students, "Their priorities are to eat, sleep, study, and get good grades. Anything in between is gravy." She adds, "They can map out a few hours to volunteer." She believes student volunteers have three advantages: 1) It helps students recognize their passion and what they are fond of; 2) It sends a message to contacts that you care about their work, and 3) It also makes you an attractive job and internship candidate.

CHAPTER 14
BRAND IDENTITY: PROFESSIONAL SELF-PROMOTION

No one can hire you if they do not know you exist. The people who best market themselves will succeed over the people with only the best skills. IACM challenges you to start thinking of yourself in the same way famous college athletes consider themselves.

Serious college athletes – with professional ambitions – are always marketing themselves to become higher draft picks in their respective sports. They know the higher their draft status, the higher their income. Take a cue from your friends on the court and gridiron who are constantly conditioning, practicing, and showcasing their skills and talents. They are persistently promoting themselves and trying to connect with industry gatekeepers in hopes of getting to the next level. You can use the same mentality and techniques to increase your stock as a first-round prospect in your desired industry.

Your mission is to distinguish yourself from your competition. Your job is to make your package of skills, education, and experiences a compelling case for your employment or acceptance into graduate or professional school. It should become what bestselling author Tony Robbins calls your magnificent obsession.

College athletes and athletic programs do a great job marketing their product. You can do likewise by maximizing your time, resources, and efforts. You can achieve the same objectives by competing, marketing yourself, and promoting yourself. Game on!

***

Competing

 "Do your work with your whole heart and you will succeed - there's so little competition."
— **Elbert Hubbard**, Writer, Philosopher

There are thousands of on-and off-campus competitions geared toward showcasing the best and brightest collegiate minds in the country. These contests cater to virtually all academic majors and professional interests. Nearly every professional organization has annual competitions (See: Appendix A). *Awards, Honors & Prizes* (Gale, Cengage Learning) is the most comprehensive single directory of awards and their donors. Use this resource to explore more opportunities.

Participating in these competitions gives you exposure to industry leaders, develops your credibility, demonstrates your competitive drive, and gives you an opportunity to size up your peers (your future job and graduate school competitors) across the country.

***

Personal Marketing Tool Kit

What is your resume' saying behind your back? Graphic artist Sonya Lowery answers that question in her book *The Secret Language of Business Cards* (Jordan Maxwell Publishing).

"When you leave a meeting or an interview, you are no longer speaking for yourself," declares Lowery, a former graphic artist and current host of World Next Door TV. "The materials you leave behind are speaking for you."

Her company's motto is, "You only get one chance to make a first impression." Lowery explains, "If you are leaving behind an unprofessional application, resume', or marketing package, it says that you are unprofessional."

Your business cards and marketing materials must communicate that you are serious, professional, and ready for business. "Legitimate marketing materials say that you are serious about your reputation and serious about having a successful career," Lowery informs.

William T. Rolack, MBA, agrees that your marketing and professional materials must be flawless. "Your resume' must be error free," counsels Rolack, who formerly served as senior director of Workforce Strategy, Diversity and Strategic Alliances for Major League Baseball in the Office of the Commissioner.

Rolack says the road to getting hired begins with a great resume'. "Use action verbs to describe what you have done at previous jobs. There are only so many times you can use 'responsible for' in a resume'. You want to talk about how you managed, facilitated, and developed various outcomes. That is what recruiters are looking for regarding action verbs."

For example, if you worked as a public relations intern for a nonprofit agency, instead of writing, "responsible for press releases, media relations, and press conferences;" Rolack encourages you to demonstrate how you managed the establishment's public image, or share how you created the agency's newsletter and attracted a significant number of subscribers. You want to communicate your value to your former and current employers. For instance, explain how your work increased the firm's media profile and led to a 12 percent increase in contributions. Include the results in accurate and straightforward terms. You can make an appointment with a career center counselor to help you construct a compelling resume'. The error-free guidance also applies to any communications (emails, texts, social media posts, and handwritten or typed correspondence).

Include the following items in your marketing toolkit:

- **APPEARANCE:** Build your professional wardrobe with black, blue, and gray business suits, skirts, dresses, or blazer sets. Include at least two white shirts and a light blue shirt. Men can buy a few solid ties from a discount department store or thrift store. Women can purchase a discrete set of accessories at the same locations.

Purchase a quality pair of black dress shoes. Maintain them with polish and wax. Invest in these must-have professional garments. They will serve you well during your college stay. Appearance also includes grooming (hair maintenance, body odor, nails, and posture.)

- **PROFESSIONAL HEADSHOT:** Your brand begins with a professional headshot. Smile and dress professionally (this varies depending on your industry). You can get a passport photo at your local drugstore or supermarket, or ask a photography student to shoot it for you. Scan or digitize it and use it on your collateral materials, LinkedIn profile, and social networking sites.

- **DOMAIN NAME:** Buy a domain name with your legal name, e.g., www. ZachRinkins.com.

- **PROFESSIONAL EMAIL:** Using a branded email offers a crisp, impressive and professional representation of yourself. Avoid using e-mail addresses with unprofessional nicknames. Human Resource professionals either throw away or plain out ignore resumes with inappropriate names. You can buy a domain for approximately $10 each year. Use this domain name as the home for your online resume site. Check out About.me, Wix.com, or Weebly.com for attractive options.

- **VIDEO BUSINESS CARD:** Develop a video business card that includes your contact information, skill sets, core competencies, and desired career paths.

- **SOCIAL MEDIA:** Facebook, Twitter, LinkedIn, and other social networking sites can be useful tools to connect with associates, contacts, and experts in your industry. Use your sites as a resource for information regarding your industry. Post helpful articles and tidbits about your industry. Also, post and re-tweet the victories of friends, fellow students, mentors and key people in your field.

Remember, do not post anything that you would not want to be published in the *New York Times*. Companies have fired and recalled employment offers from employees deemed socially irresponsible. Remember, if you put it online it is hard to take it back.

- **PROFESSIONAL DOCUMENTS:** Marketing materials also include professional documents like applications for grants, scholarships, internships, fellowships, and graduate school. These documents communicate your desire and worthiness for an institution or opportunity. You want to give yourself an earlier deadline to complete these items and recruit people to edit them and offer suggestions.

- **ENERGY AND ATTITUDE:** People are often sizing you up without your knowledge. People can also judge you based on the vibe or feelings you project. That makes having an upbeat attitude, positive and respectful demeanor, and social and physical graces immensely critical. Reading Dale Carnegie's *How to Win Friends and Influence People* (Simon and Schuster) will help you develop techniques to project your best energy and attitude.

Anything that has your name on it should say great things about you. Produce collateral materials that market and summarize your background, talents, and abilities. These materials help introduce you and showcase your skills to the gatekeepers of your industry. Always present yourself in a professional manner. Perception is everything! In nearly all occasions, people will treat you how they perceive you. After you have developed your marketing materials, you are now ready to proceed further.

***
Promoting Yourself

❝ *"Self-promotion is a leadership and political skill that is critical to master to navigate the realities of the workplace and position you for success."*
— **Bonnie Marcus**, Author, *The Politics of Promotion: How High-Achieving Women Get Ahead and Stay Ahead* (Wiley) ❞

Whether you realize it, you are selling yourself to people and opportunities every day. American business executive Beth Comstock says, "You can't sell anything if you can't tell anything." As you go to more networking events and conferences and start winning competitions, scholarships, and internships, make sure you keep your network and industry insiders aware of your accomplishments.

You can do this by skillfully and tactfully promoting yourself. Do not be afraid to shamelessly plug your wins to professors, school administrators, career center staff, and your network. It gives you an opportunity to educate people about your goals, accomplishments, and timeline. It is best to use press releases and alerts, emails, conversations, websites, and social media to get your message to your network and solicit their support.

PRESS RELEASES AND ALERTS
You can hire someone on Fiverr.com or work with a communications student or professor to help you construct a professional press release. Upon completion, send it to the following sources:

- Newspapers, television and radio stations in your college city and hometown
- Professional group and organization listservs
- www.HelpAReporter.com
- The public relations departments of your professional and social organizations

- Recruitment, public relations, and human resource departments of all the companies you are courting for internships or employment
- The admissions office, contacts, and key employees at prospective graduate or professional schools
- Use PRLog.com to distribute press releases worldwide at no cost
- Former internship supervisors and company co-workers who may be able to place your story in their newsletters
- Your mentors, friends, and family members
- Your social media platforms, especially LinkedIn

E-Mails

Use a soft touch when talking to former colleagues and prospective job and graduate school contacts. You want it to feel like you are *sharing* and not bragging or pushing the information. You can send an email to your former supervisors that reads:

Example 1:

Mrs. Thomas:

Thank you for helping me accomplish the following (see attached).

I could not have done it without your guidance. Feel free to share with the communications department, if you like.

Sincerely,

Zach

You can send an email to your professors and university or organization contacts that says:

Example 2:

Dr. Miller:

I hope all is well with you. I wanted to bring this (see attached) to your attention.

I was happy to represent the university at the NBSE convention. Feel free to share with the communications department, if you like.

Sincerely,

Zach

All communications must be error free, discreet, and professional. This creates an effective formula to inform others.

You can also use your email signature to highlight your accomplishments and educate your audience about your graduation timeline. It might appear as:

EXAMPLE A
Sincerely,
Zach Rinkins
Emerging Electrical Engineer
Graduating, August 2020
Zach@IAmCollegeMaterial.com
www.IAmCollegeMaterial.com

EXAMPLE B
Sincerely,
Zach Rinkins
Fall 2020 MBA Candidate
"2019 Rice Business Plan
Competition Winner"
Zach@IAmCollegeMaterial.com
www.IAmCollegeMaterial.com

EXAMPLE C
Sincerely,
Zach Rinkins
Computer Science Job Prospect
Graduating April 2021
View my portfolio on LinkedIn @
www.linkedin.com/in/zachrinkins/

In Example A, you are informing everyone with whom you communicate that you are poised to graduate with a degree in engineering. In Example B, you are telling receivers that you are graduating with a graduate degree and won a popular entrepreneurship competition. In Example C, you are letting them know when you graduate, that you are looking for professional opportunities, and how they can access your portfolio. Use the best information combination to help you advance your ambitions.

CONVERSATIONS

It is helpful to know with whom you are talking and how they might help you. That is why it is important to research your industry and its professionals. You can research a person by using Google Alerts and Google News. You can also use LinkedIn to find out to whom they are connected.

For example, before asking your question during a professional forum, you might say:

EXAMPLE 1:

Greetings, fellow members of the Society of Professional Journalists. I am Zach Rinkins, a graduating senior from Florida A&M University with a passion for broadcast journalism. (Then, ask your question.)

In conversations with professional contacts, you could say:

EXAMPLE 2:

I am so excited about graduating with my biology education degree. I am looking for opportunities to work at middle schools. Would you please let me know if you have any contacts or resources that could help me achieve this aim?

Or

EXAMPLE 3:

Hello, Dr. Jenkins. I met you last week at the department's spring mixer for biology students. I saw on

LinkedIn that you are connected to Dr. Susan Mathis at the University of Illinois College of Medicine. I am poised to graduate with a 3.7 GPA and applied there for medical school. Would you be willing to connect me with her?

Knowing to whom you are speaking, how they might assist you, and the quality of your connection with them has a significant impact on how you converse with them.

WEBSITES

Many firms are using web-based outlets to recruit and vet prospects. Post your resume' and a basic cover letter on Indeed.com, SimplyHired.com, Recruiter.com, Idealist.org, and others. There are even sites that specialized in certain industries and sectors.

SOCIAL MEDIA

Social media is a useful tool to let your network and others know what you are doing and inform them about your needs. Use social media promotional tactics with the following outlets:

LINKEDIN:

LinkedIn is strictly for business purposes. Limit posts to networking and advancing your professional ambitions. You can also apply for jobs here.

- After posting your resume' and portfolio, you can highlight yourself on your LinkedIn profile as a person looking for opportunities.
- Make posts on your other social media profiles asking for feedback on your LinkedIn Profile. This helps expose your resume' to others.
- Include your education, competition awards, publications, skill sets, and software proficiencies.
- Post requests for information about internships, jobs, scholarships, and other opportunities.

- Search for alumni that may be affiliated with companies, admissions administrators, and hiring recruiters in which you may be interested.

FACEBOOK AND TWITTER

Facebook is for socializing. You do not want to overly promote yourself. Be skillful and consider Dr. Michael Lomax's advice about crafting attractive information that features personal narratives (See: Free Money: Grants and Scholarships).

Other strategies could include:

- Posting pictures you take with industry experts and contacts.
- Posting requests for information about internships, jobs, scholarships, and other opportunities.
- Viewing research about various software and skill sets needed for your career, then crafting a story showcasing your mastery of the items.

For example, a post could read:

> You can master anything if you hang in there. This new Adobe Premiere Pro software was kicking my butt. I studied, struggled, stumbled, and now I am editing videos. #YouCanDoIt! #KeepGoing

> *Or*

> Countdown to JD! This semester was very challenging. Mastering torts, procedures, and legal writing were grueling and exciting at the same time. I have three months until graduation. #FutureLawyer #SouthernUniversityLaw #Fall2020

You can always ask for help with identifying opportunities:

Good day, all. I am a graduating software engineering student looking for job and internship opportunities. Please inbox me if you have any contacts or leads.

All of these posts let people know your skills, needs, and graduation timeline. You can also use social media sites to share and repost the victories of influencers in your desired industry.

CHAPTER 15
CRAFTING A BLUEPRINT FOR CAREER SUCCESS

> " *"The price of success is hard work, dedication to the job at hand, and the determination that whether we win or lose, we have applied the best of ourselves to the task at hand."*
> — **Vince Lombardi**, Legendary Football Coach " "

Everything you encounter is nurturing you for life after college. General education and elective courses help you appreciate the mundane, abstract, and intellectual qualities of life. Prerequisite courses equip you to master the upper-level courses necessary to develop professional competence. All of your professional, internship, and volunteer experiences get you ready for your first real professional job after graduation. It is one of the most important decisions you will make in your career.

Morgan Stanley's Carla Harris says, "You have to understand what success means to you." She advises you to define it for yourself and to go after it aggressively. "You have to be the architect of your agenda. You need to understand exactly why you are going to a particular company and why you are taking that particular seat," Harris explains. "The seat is the content of your job, and the house is where you are doing it."

Yvette Birner, a 20-year human resources professional, embraces that sentiment. "While considering different job offers, recent graduates must pay attention to what experiences they want to get from their first job because those experiences will either help or hurt your future career opportunities and compensation," offers Birner, who has served in various at capacities at Brocade, ALCF, and Apple, Inc.

It is equally important to start your career in growing industry sectors (See: From BA to Payday! Majors and Consequences). These industries are more likely to offer higher compensation packages and professional development programs.

RLJ Companies chairman Robert L. Johnson says doing so allows you to benefit from the growth and stability of emerging markets and opportunities. Johnson, who built two billion-dollar companies and several hundred-million-dollar firms, said, "I see three opportunities that I am convinced are going to grow dramatically. Those opportunities are in health and health services, leisure (hospitality and tourism), and technology. Being able to compete effectively in these areas opens up vast doors of opportunity," Johnson advises to young people considering various professional opportunities.

In addition to knowing your career ambitions, Birner says compensation is an integral factor when determining your first job:

> "Your first salary is going to make or break your whole future. Once you already work for a company, it is very rare for them to increase your salary beyond 3 to 5 percent," warns Birner, a graduate of Santa Clara University. "Your salary follows you everywhere. It sets the compensation trajectory for your current company and future job opportunities because potential employers are going to ask you what your last salary was. Then, they typically give you 15 or 20 percent more than that."

Knowing your appropriate value can be a daunting task for some soon-to-be graduates. Birner admits that your value differs depending on the industry, environment, and company. She likens the situation to the National Football League:

> "On football teams, some positions are more valuable than others. The entry salary for those positions is very different. It doesn't mean those positions aren't compensated well. There are just certain positions where you go through five different people in the course of time. During that same period, you may have just one

quarterback. In this example, the quarterback is more valuable and has flexibility because they are almost irreplaceable. You become more valuable when you have skill sets and experiences that a company values."

There are other considerations when determining whether a job is a good fit for you (See: Internship Success for the Emerging Professional). Location is a major consideration because it has an enormous impact on your taxes and cost of living.

TAXES

A $50,000 a year salary is not the same for every location. For example, a person living in California who earns a $50,000 annual salary is paid $1,388.71 bi-weekly before fringe benefits. Conversely, a person in Texas with the same annual salary is paid $1,481.21 bi-weekly before fringe benefits.

COST OF LIVING

Investopedia.com defines cost of living as the amount of money needed to sustain a certain level of living, including basic expenses such as housing, food, taxes and health care. It is more expensive to live in San Francisco, California than Dallas, Texas. According to CNN's Cost of Living Calculator, a Dallas resident earning $50,000 would have to earn $90,612 to maintain the same cost of living in San Francisco. A Dallas resident with that salary can afford to purchase a starter house. A San Francisco resident is more likely to live with one or more roommates.

Birner advises students to research their industry and the company to find out total compensation components like perquisites, investment options, and fringe benefits. "If you are a new graduate and an organization is offering you 401k matching, stock options, and restricted stock units as part of your package, you have to take into account how that affects your long-term goals," she counsels. "You have to do your own research to find out what is available to you."

IACM identified several resources that can help you determine a fair salary:

- **GOVERNMENT JOBS:** Government sector financial information is public information. You can search Google or the entity's budget department to retrieve this information. You can also request copies of the budget from the entity's Public Information Department. This will enable you to research salaries of people in your desired or similar position.

- **NOT-FOR-PROFITS:** Not-for-profit jobs must report their highest wages and provide access to their annual reports (Form 990). GuideStar (www. www.guidestar.org) is a great place to obtain the reports. You can also research organizations that are similar to your prospective employer for compensation clues.

- **PRIVATE SECTOR JOBS:** You have to do more research to find out competitive income rates for these positions. You can start by searching online or in the classified section for similar jobs and duties. Also, see what competitors are paying your counterparts.

- **YOUR NETWORK:** Ask your professors, mentors, alumni in your profession and professional association members to help you determine a fair salary.

There are two reasons employers do not pay all employees the same salary: 1) Because different employees and positions are valued differently; and 2) Because some employees are not effective negotiators.   Other variables like educational background, experience, and your time with a company will affect your salary.

Birner encourages emerging professionals to manage their expectations. "Your job and your lifestyle do not necessarily have to match. You may want to live in a glamorous location and enjoy a certain lifestyle, but it is not your job's responsibility to match that expectation. Most people should not expect to graduate from college and then purchase a house, live on their own, have a lot of excess money to travel the world, and have a fabulous wardrobe. It happens for a few people, but not everyone."

Additionally, Birner says you want to know the salary range before you interview for a position. "Ask the recruiter or HR representative the salary range. It is good to know the range because it helps you know where you stand. Your ability to negotiate depends on where you fall in that range," she points out. "You want to end up at the higher end of the range."

Birner recommends three tactics for job negotiation success:

- **REMAIN FOCUSED:** "Do your research on what you want to get out of the situation. Never go into a negotiation situation without knowing exactly what you want to get out of it."

- **REMAIN PROFESSIONAL:** "Establish a rapport with the person and never come off curt and arrogant. Have a conversation with the recruiter and remain professional. There is a fine line between being confident and arrogant. You never want to come across as trying to prove that you know more than the recruiter does."

- **DON'T BE AFRAID TO ASK FOR MORE:** "You can always ask for more. You don't have to necessarily have a reason. Knowing the range helps you know how much you can ask for."

The deal making and negotiation processes have a beginning and an ending. Get all important details in writing. Do not over-negotiate or pointlessly extend the process when you have a great offer. Close the deal with class and style. Make the experience pleasurable by staying responsive with your recruiter. Also, send a thank you note.

CHAPTER 16
COMMENCEMENT: FINISH STRONG

❝ *"Man's future is largely in his own hands. In his higher brain, he has an organ with which he can successfully solve all his major problems, but he cannot derive full benefits from his organ unless he educates it – a matter nature has left almost entirely to him."*
— **W. Montague Cobb, M.D., Ph.D.,**
Anatomist, Historian, and Anthropologist **❞**

Seminal scholar Dr. W. Montague Cobb promised that through education we have the potential to solve all of our problems. Conversely, without education, we cannot even see the problems much less solve them.

Through reading this book, you have gained critical insight into understanding how to take responsibility for your future, prepare for your future, minimize your challenges, and maximize your opportunities. As an emerging professional, you have been preparing yourself for this moment.

Dr. Price Cobbs, author of *My American Life: From Rage to Entitlement* (Atria) affirms:

> "You are entitled to success. Entitlement is focusing on what you can do, not what the world can do for you. Entitlement is an understanding that you are entitled to all the things you aspire to, all the things you prepared yourself for, all of the things you are qualified for and of which you are capable."

Once you accept that you are entitled to success, there is only one thing left to do – "step out and jump," says hip-hop impresario David Banner. "God is not a cruel God. God would not torture you by allowing you to think or feel strongly about something that you could not fulfill. The question is: are you man or woman enough to make it happen?"

Understand that graduation is not the finish line. It is your starting line! The word "commence" literally means to start. While in college, maximize every resource and opportunity at your disposal to create an action plan for a prosperous and fulfilling future that excites you and serves others. Be strategic. Start NOW! Effectively educate yourself so you can fully capitalize on your potential and see life's possibilities. Your future depends on you. You can do it. **REMEMBER, YOU ARE COLLEGE MATERIAL!**

APPENDIX A
Professional Organizations

- American Pre-Veterinary Medical Association: www.APVMA.org
- American Psychological Association: www.APA.org
- American Society of Mechanical Engineers: www.ASME.org
- Association of Black Psychologists: www.ABPsi.org
- Association of Latino Professionals for America: www.ALPFA.org
- National Association of Black Accountants: www.NABAinc.org
- National Association Black Journalists: http: www.nabj.org
- National Black MBA Association: www.NBMBAA.org
- National Association of Social Workers: www.NASWDC.org
- National Society of Black Engineers: www.NSBE.org
- National Society of Professional Engineers: www.NSPE.org
- Phi Alpha Delta Law Fraternity, International: www.PAD.org
- Public Relations Student Society of America: www.PRSSA.PRSA.org
- Society of Hispanic Professional Engineers: www.SHPE.org
- Society of Human Resource Management: www.SHRM.org
- Society of Professional Journalists: www.SPJ.org

The Gale Company publishes an *Encyclopedia of Associations: National Organizations of the U.S. (EA)*, a directory featuring all the associations in the U.S.

APPENDIX B
Group Study Resource

Study Group Resources

LOUISIANA STATE UNIVERSITY STUDY GROUP STARTER KIT
www.lsu.edu/students/cas/files/StudyGroupStarterKit_color_re
v1.pdf

Graduate Admission Tests & Accreditation Resources

GRADUATE PROGRAM ADMISSIONS TESTS
In nearly all cases, graduate schools require students to pass
admission tests for consideration. Tests include:

- Dental Admission Test (DAT), for prospective dental
  school students
- Graduate Management Admission Test (GMAT), for
  prospective graduate business school students
- Graduate Record Examination (GRE), for prospective
  graduate school students
- Law School Admission Test (LSAT), for prospective law
  school students
- Medical College Admission Test (MCAT), for prospective
  medical school students
- Pharmacy College Admission Test (PCAT), for
  prospective graduate pharmacy school students

COLLEGE, SCHOOL, AND PROGRAM ACCREDITING BODIES

Professional and graduate schools often maintain separate
academic accreditations from their undergraduate
counterparts. Regional bodies such as the Southern Association
of Colleges and Schools (SACS) designate these U.S. Department
of Education-recognized accreditations that allow students to

secure federal financial aid and sit for professional exams (e.g., engineering, architecture, medical, law, and nursing certifications). Without regional accreditation, schools are not eligible to issue financial aid. Additionally, graduates cannot sit for professional and credentialing exams. If you are pursuing a career in a highly regulated profession, you want to limit yourself to schools accredited by the appropriate bodies:

- Post-secondary education programs in applied science, computing, engineering, and engineering technology are accredited by the Accreditation Board for Engineering and Technology, Inc. (ABET).
- Business schools are accredited by either the Association to Advance Collegiate Schools of Business (AACSB) or the Accreditation Council for Business Schools and Programs (ACBSP).
- Dental schools are accredited by the Commission on Dental Accreditation (DCA).
- Law Schools are accredited by the American Bar Association (ABA).
- Medical schools are accredited by the Liaison Committee on Medical Education (LCME).
- Pharmacy schools are accredited by the Accreditation Council for Pharmacy Education (ACPE).
- Nursing schools are accredited by the Commission on Collegiate Nursing Education (CCNE) or the Accreditation Commission for Education in Nursing (ACEN).
- Pharmacy schools are accredited by the Accreditation Council for Pharmacy Education (ACPE).

APPENDIX C
Problem Solving Resource

UNIVERSITY OF MICHIGAN'S
THOUGHTS ON PROBLEM SOLVING SITE

http://www.umich.edu/~elements/5e/probsolv/index.htm

APPENDIX D
Internship Resources

THE CONGRESSIONAL BLACK CAUCUS FOUNDATION, INC. (CBCF): is a nonprofit, nonpartisan public policy research and educational institute. The foundation sponsors several internship programs including:

- CBCF Emerging Leaders Internship Program
- CBCF Communications Internship Program
- CBCF Summer Congressional Internship Program
- Pathways to the C-Suite Internship Program.

Log on to www.CBCFinc.org/internships/ for more information.

DISNEY PROFESSIONAL INTERNSHIPS: Are available in a wide range of majors and durations. The possibilities are endless. Internships are paid and may include housing and relocation assistance. Eligibility and qualifications vary by position. Visit www.profinterns.disneycareers.com for more information.

EXPLORE MICROSOFT INTERNSHIP PROGRAM: Is for current college undergraduate minority students pursuing a degree in computer science or software engineering. The 12-week program is open to women and minorities (African American, Native American, and Hispanic). The program provides students hands-on experience in software development and exposure to the field of computer science, computer engineering, or related technical areas. Log on to www.careers.microsoft.com for more information.

GOLDMAN SACHS GROUP, INC.: Is a leading global investment banking, securities and investment management firm that provides a wide range of financial services to a substantial and diversified client base that includes corporations, financial institutions, governments, and individuals. The company offers numerous internships in various disciplines. For more information, visit_www.goldmansachs.com/careers/students-and-graduates/.

INROADS: Was founded with the mission to develop and place talented underserved youth in business and industry, and prepare them for corporate and community leadership. Visit www.Inroads.org for more information.

THE NASCAR DIVERSITY INTERNSHIP PROGRAM: Identifies and engages top student talent across the country's best colleges and universities. In addition to NASCAR, the 10-week summer program partners with key stakeholders to widen employment opportunities for young professionals, including sponsors, teams, racetracks, and agencies. These paid internships include focus areas such as licensing, communications, marketing, engineering, public affairs, diversity affairs, sales, sponsorships and event planning, among others. The program provides stipends for interns in Daytona Beach, Florida, and Charlotte, North Carolina. For more information, visit www.NASCARdiversity.com.

NCAA DIVISION III ETHNIC MINORITY AND WOMEN'S INTERNSHIP GRANT PROGRAM: Is a two-year grant program that provides funding for entry-level administrative positions at NCAA Division III schools and conference offices to encourage access, recruitment, selection and the long-term success of ethnic minorities and women. During each year of grant funding, the NCAA provides $20,100 to support the salary of the hired intern and $3,000 in professional development funding. Recipients are required to provide a $3,700 minimum in-kind gift for each year of the grant. Apply at www.ncaa.org.

SEO CAREER: Is a professional development and internship program targeting talented Black, Hispanic, and Native American undergrads for internships in business, finance, and technology. SEO Career provides the education, development, growth, and experience needed to gain a competitive advantage to launch your career. Participants receive free career prep resources, training, and coaching to land a paid summer internship and ultimately to secure a full-time job offer in business, finance, or technology. Summer internships pay up to $1,300 per week. More than 80 percent of SEO Career interns were offered full-time jobs at the end of their internships – at either their host company or another SEO Career partner. Apply at www.seocareer.org.

The organization also has **SEO Law**, the only program of its kind to offer talented incoming law school students of color a unique opportunity to intern with a top law firm during the summer before law school. For 30 years, SEO Law has served as a pipeline linking talented, underrepresented minority pre-law students to PAID internships at elite global law firms. More than 1,200 interns have gone through the SEO Law internship program since 1986. Log on to www.seocareer.org/law/about/ for more information.

YEAR UP: Is an intensive training program that helps urban young adults increase their technical skills and prepare for a career in information technology. It also places students in internships at top companies. Visit www.YearUp.org, to find more information about the program.

I Am College Material

"Empowering students with a competitive advantage in college, career, and life."

Zach Rinkins is an award-winning speaker and author on a mission to help students, parents, and educators close the achievement gap by equipping students with tools to maximize their college experience. Zach draws from his experiences as a college administrator, educator, and journalist to help audiences accomplish their goals. I Am College Material! (IACM) is a suite of turnkey multimedia content that offers practical solutions covering virtually everything from registration to graduation. This material is perfect for orientations, student government, Greek life, Upward Bound/TRIO, leadership, honors, student affairs, graduation and career services events. IACM includes the following presentations and workshops:

- **I Am College Material!**
- **Are You Ready for a 21st Century Career?**
- **It's Payday! Taking Your Finances by F.O.R.C.E.!**
- **Diversity: Owning Your Personal Power!**
- **Life, Liberty, and the Pursuit of an Education!**
- **Realities in College Relationships**
- **Honey, We Sent the Kids to College! What Do We Do Now?** (*for parents*) **and so much more.**

These impactful experiences help students go from inspiration to implementation. Let's find out how we can work together to achieve your university's student retention and graduation goals as you also work to close the achievement gap. Email info@IAmCollegeMaterial.com to inquire about Zach Rinkins' availability to serve your audience. Log on to www.IAmCollegeMaterial.com for more information.

www.IAmCollegeMaterial.com

87606229R00124

Made in the USA
Columbia, SC
23 January 2018